Under the Paw

BOOTSY

PABLO

Brewer

RALPH

Daisy

Monty

Under the Paw

Confessions of a
Cat Man

TOM COX

SIMON &
SCHUSTER

London · New York · Sydney · Toronto

A CBS COMPANY

First published in Great Britain in 2008 by
Simon & Schuster UK Ltd
A CBS COMPANY

1 3 5 7 9 10 8 6 4 2

Simon & Schuster UK Ltd
Africa House
64–78 Kingsway
London WC2B 6AH

www.simonsays.co.uk

Simon & Schuster Australia
Sydney

Illustrations courtesy of Edie Mullen

A CIP catalogue record for this book
is available from the British Library.

ISBN: 978-1-84737-141-6

Typeset in Goudy by M Rules
Printed and bound in Great Britain by
Mackays of Chatham plc

For Dee, my loving wife, and Flump,
a cat I met on the Internet.

Acknowledgements

Special thanks to Dee, Simon Trewin (uber-agent), my excellent editor Angela Herlihy, who could hardly have had a worse time to be working on a cat book, Jo and Mick, Trowse Jen, Simon and Carolyn, Bob and Rosemary, and to all the readers of http://littlecatdiaries.blogspot.com. I must also express particular gratitude to The Bear, who, in a quiet moment when Shipley and Bootsy aren't trying to muscle in on his Certified Reconditioned box, will no doubt read this and file it away for future reference. The rest of you know who you are. Or maybe you don't. Whatever the case, you've been treating this house like a hotel for too long, and it's high time you started pulling your weight.

'Thrown, as you must be, incessantly among loose and immoral bohemians, you will find in this cat an example of upright conduct which cannot but act as an antidote to the poison cup of temptation.'

– P. G. Wodehouse, 'The Story of Webster'

'Who's the cat that won't cop out when there's danger all about?'

– Isaac Hayes, 'Theme from Shaft'

Contents

My Cat Timeline

Puss (1971–5)

Felix (1972–89)

Tabs (1986–7)

Monty (aka The Ponce) (1987–98)

Daisy (aka The Slink) (1991–2007)

The Bear (1995–present)

Janet (1997–present)

Brewer (2001–2002)

Ralph (née Prudence) (2001–present)

Shipley (2001–present)

Pablo (2005–present)

Bootsy (2005–present)

Prologue

First of all, the facts. My name is Tom, I am crazy about cats, and, just under thirty-three years ago, I was almost certainly responsible for the death of one.

Everyone knows about Mad Cat Lady. She's a social cliché, a cautionary tale, a character that, when she started to pop up in cartoon form on *The Simpsons*, was so instantly resonant that she didn't have to be named or introduced. She is the childless woman who lets her cat obsession take over her life, to the detriment of domestic and, finally, personal hygiene. In truth, as a stereotype she seems a little unfair. After all, there is no firmly established Mad Dog Man to counterbalance her. The subtext of all this seems to be that a Man's Best Friend will help him see out the autumn of his life with dignity, while a woman's will help her see out hers alone in a supermarket, giving off a slightly mildewy odour, pushing a trolley containing only a malt loaf, some hairnets, a packet of wafer thin ham and twenty-four cans of Felix. Mad Cat Man is a less widely reported phenomenon, but I am here to tell you that he exists, and has the capacity to be at least as obsessive as his female counterpart.

Of course, I am not *really* crazy. My house might get a bit smelly when I haven't vacuumed or checked under the sofa for a few days, but it is by no means a health hazard. I did once put a necktie on one of my cats when he was asleep, but I have never bought one of them an item of clothing and I don't call them 'fur babies'. I do, however, currently own six of them, which, in maintenance terms, can be a little bit like living with half a dozen miniature versions of Mariah Carey. No doubt, by the time you've read this, another little bundle of narcissistic fur will have wandered in off the street, decided it likes what it sees, and parked itself on one of the purpose-made hammocks that hang from the radiators in my house. I will probably even learn to ignore the obscene snorty scronking sound it makes while it cleans its bottom. It has happened before, and I'm sure it will happen again.

Telling you this feels more taboo than it ought to. What is it about cats that makes so many men suspicious of them, and so many people suspicious of the men who like them? What do they think their cat-fancying brethren are doing: hatching little furry plots for the downfall of our gender?

Being a heterosexual man and admitting to another hetero-sexual man that you like cats can feel a little like telling him that you still sleep alongside your childhood collection of teddy bears, or that you think his knitted waistcoat is 'cute'. Yet the statistics simply don't match up to the popular image of the Cat Man as society's outcast: there are currently more than 9 million cats in the UK, probably over a billion in the world itself, and it would be foolish to believe that, even as we speak, a sizeable portion of them are not currently being fed overindulgent snacks and tickled under their chins by men as well as women.

Who are we Cat Blokes, then? Are we real-life Dr Evils? Pensioners in long johns with hair in our home-made ginger nuts and urine on our sofas? Transvestite second-hand bookshop owners? Are we (claw, hiss, spit) *metrosexuals*? Maybe we are, but we are also great American novelists (Mark Twain), demon-fighters (*Buffy the Vampire Slayer* star Anthony Head), mathematicians (Isaac Newton) and world leaders (Winston Churchill). You can try to put us in a box, but, much like our four-legged allies, we'll escape, insouciantly shake ourselves down, and do our own thing. Some of us hide our cat love from the world. Some of us take things a little too far. Some of us are just normal blokes who see nothing emasculating about wanting to spend time with the world's most popular household pet, and our cat love does not serve as a metaphor or a crutch.

That said, some of us also have what a psychoanalyst might call 'a cat history'. To trace mine, you really would have to go right back to the beginning. And I mean the *very* beginning.

When I ask myself how my life became so completely dominated by cats, I repeatedly come back to two pivotal moments. One occurred in a dark rural garden in 1998 and seemed pivotal in a different way at the time. The other occurred in early 1975, in an even darker place, at a time when 'pivotal', like all other words, was meaningless.

Not having been blessed with the ability to see through amniotic fluid and skin, I never got to meet Puss, the first cat in my life, in person. From my parents' recollections of her, I tend to picture her as half Pac Mog, half gremlin, chomping and clawing everything in her path in a furious plume of smoke before retiring to the eves to make tiny cackling noises and plot her next move. 'SHE WOULD HAVE HAD YOUR HAND OFF IN A SECOND,' my dad has frequently explained. For many years it did not occur to me to question the veracity of this, or the wisdom of my parents' decision to have her put to sleep in the fifth month of my mum's pregnancy.

When I was growing up, The Legend of Puss was an indelible part of Cox mythology, right up there with The Legend of the Time I Almost Died of a Burst Appendix and the Time My Dad Bought A Morris Minor for a Tenner. It has only been recently that I've looked at the photographs depicting an undersized, sandy-coloured cat, and noticed that they don't quite seem to tally with the oft-repeated stories of shredded wrists and fleeing postmen. And what, I wonder, of Felix, my parents' other not stupendously originally named 1970s moggy, an animal best known for her gentle, pliable nature and pillow soft fur? According to my feline family tree, Felix was born in 1972. How did such an innocent creature manage to not only survive Puss's iron rule for two full years, but give birth as well? Wouldn't Puss have chewed her kittens to pulpy masses and spat them at the milkman?

As my mum remembers it, Puss had always had a mile-wide mean streak, but after my parents found her on the road outside their house, her back legs crushed in a hit and run, she became a cat out of hell. While Puss would walk again, her rear half never fully recovered from the accident, leaving her pained and furious. In the end, though, it was my impending arrival that was responsible for booking her final trip to the vets.

'You would have done the same thing, if you were getting ready to give birth for the first time,' says my mum. I find this hard to believe, but, since I don't plan to get knocked up any time soon, I am unlikely to find out.

Whether the millstone of Puss's death was responsible for my lifelong need to be around cats – to invite them in to soil my furniture, to spoil them, to let them push me around – I cannot say for certain. It is entirely possible that, had Puss survived my gestation, I would be sitting here writing this with one less eye and a Dobermann pinscher curled up at my feet. Whatever the case, when you grow up burdened with the knowledge of having been the catalyst for an animal's death, it's probably going to help to shape who you are, whether you like it or not.

Add to this an appropriate first name and initials – I'd been at primary school all of twenty minutes when one of my classmates started singing the *Top Cat* theme tune ('close friends get to call him TC!') – and the die is well on the way to being cast. Another theory regarding why I love cats so much is that I have always liked a challenge. There is also the possibility that, when you live in the back-of-beyond, ten miles from your nearest schoolfriend, you take what company you can get, even if the most positive feedback you can get from that company is a grudging half-purr and a disdainfully proffered chin.

A typical summer day in 1978 at our three-bed semi in the north-east Midlands countryside would have found the 3-year-old me eating soil in the back garden, trying to befriend Gordon Witchell's cows in the back field, or practising my before-their-time homoeopathic massaging techniques on Felix. My mum's child substitute must have breathed a sigh of relief when Puss mysteriously 'went to the furry retirement village' and never came back, but her respite was brief. If Felix looks nervous in many of the photos of her from my toddlerhood, it does not take a Zoology PhD to work out why – at least, not once you have spotted the small, clammy pair of hands frequently reaching out into the edge of the frame.

Not long after my fourth summer on the planet, she

decided she'd had enough of being chased under furniture and treated like a pre-school stress-relief ball and went to live next door with a nice old lady called Flo, whom my dad claimed was just approaching her 134th birthday. There she stayed for the next three years, until Flo died and her house was bought by a retired alcoholic doctor: a man more likely to mistake the long-suffering Felix for an unusually furry black and white beer towel than ply her with titbits.

By the time Felix came back to live with us, I'd found other interests to occupy my time – making dens in the woods by the newly closed neighbouring coalmine, performing stunts on my BMX, and having my one, precious *Star Wars* figurine liquefied by a terrifying 9-year-old from three doors away called Ian Saw. But Felix remained circumspect around me, particularly at times when I happened to have haircare equipment upon my person.

Depending on whether I'm feeling self-pitying or upbeat at the time, I can look upon my early childhood as either a classic example of only-child rural isolation, or a classic example of pass-the-parcel, post-hippy urban utopia. I always liked the look of the place my parents referred to in slightly scornful tones as 'suburbia', but as I remained unfamiliar with its inhabitants, I knew it only as the place where my mum and dad's jalopies sometimes broke down on the way back from the inner city school where my mum taught and I was a pupil.

Claremont Primary School was an institution that seemed to embody a lot of the best things about the hippy era without being self-consciously progressive or predominantly middle class. Here, I churned butter and played 'Dungeons & Dragons' with kids called Aseef, Esme, Danny and Sorrel, before going home to read Roald Dahl's *The Fantastic Mr Fox* and Dick King-Smith's *The Mouse Butcher* for the umpteenth time, and hunt for water beetles for my DIY garden pond. The gummy, idyllic class pictures of me and my multi-ethnic, socially diverse friends from Claremont, with our straggly hair and towelling sweatshirts, tell one story of the first ten years of my life, but the photos from my back garden in Brinsley and my holidays from the same period probably tell the more accurate one. 'Ooh yes!' I say to my mum, as she gets the old albums out. 'Here's me with that boxer dog, Billy, that I befriended on that camp-site in Dorset – the one whose owners took me to the funfair in Weymouth . . . And those Muscovy ducks that came in the kitchen when we stayed in Bath . . . And there's that black and white pair of kittens we met on the campsite in Italy, the ones we called Evil and Knievel . . . And that German kid who I played table tennis with, the one who got rushed to hospital when he banged his head on the bottom of the swimming pool.'

These photos speak of a socially active childhood, but one where all new acquaintances were greeted with equal enthusiasm, whether they happened to be human or animal. I would estimate in about 40 per cent of them I'm holding, or somewhere in the nearby vicinity of, a cat.

Given my alarming aptitude for remembering the names of other people's pets from over two decades ago, I'm some-what abashed to say that I recall relatively little about Tabs, my second cat. I am certain this owes nothing to lack of care or affection, just as I am certain I had never before experi-enced anything approaching the gut-wrenching devastation I felt when, while making her way across the road to meet us in her customary, enthusiastic early-evening way, not long after her first birthday, she was hit by a car.

Her death was mercifully instant, leaving her looking peaceful, with just a single, tiny spot of blood beside her on the kerb. I still have a clear image of a wobbly lipped 12-year-old me explaining to Mrs Deeth, my maths teacher, about the tragic event that had prevented me from doing my homework (Mrs Deeth had a stern reputation, but Wayne Smith and Beau O'Dowd on the back row really were very unfair to call her 'Mrs Death' – she was actually very understanding).

My parents decided the best remedy for my grief was a visit to the Burton Joyce Cats Rescue Centre, where I formed an unmistakable bond with Monty, a sinewy, white and sandy-coloured chap – and I use the word 'chap' pointedly – with a look of mischief in his eye.

On the way home, as the smell of Monty's first bowel evacuation of the evening mingled with that of our takeaway curry, I began to feel like a traitor. Choking back the tears, I explained to my mum that I might be making a mistake trying to 'replace' Tabs so hastily. Much as they tore at my innards, these sentiments somewhat started to dissipate later that evening, when Monty started making gargling noises and running up and down the living room curtains.

Monty was one of those animals who come along every so often that seem a little more patrician than the rest of their species. He was the kind of cat that even lifelong catophobes could not bring themselves to loathe. Wild animals smaller than a pheasant feared him, other cats wanted to be him, divorced book group members with hennaed hair wanted to be with him. When I looked into his eyes, I saw something wild, yet controlled.

If Monty had had his own theme tune, it would either have been 'You've Got a Friend' by Carole King, or 'Theme from Shaft' by Isaac Hayes. He'd once prowled across the roof outside my bedroom while I'd been listening to the latter, and its funky string arrangements and lyrics about 'a complicated man' and 'the cat that won't cop out when there's danger all about' had seemed apt. Not, of course, that Monty would, in the words of Hayes, ever have been 'the man who would risk his neck for his brother man'. He was, after all, a cat, and wasn't going to transcend the self-absorbed limits of his species. But if he could have done, I'm sure he would have given it a go, provided it didn't involve venturing anywhere too damp.

After his initial, uncharacteristically unrestrained and alarmingly literal curtain raiser, Monty soon got down to business, outlining his primary requirements as a member of our household. These ran as follows:

1. The promise that I would not, on any account, attempt to transform him into a lap cat.
2. A strict 'No Hairdryers within fifty Feet' policy.
3. Thrice-weekly – at the very least – helpings of chicken breast (uncooked).
4. Permission to drink freely from the well of life – and the upstairs loo – without any snide comments regarding hygiene.
5. A promise that I would not react jealously or posses-sively, should his affections stray elsewhere, and know that, no matter how many milkmen/schoolfriends/members of the medical profession he rubbed himself against, I would always ultimately be the Important One.
6. That I would stick to the classic 'one-two' format – a high 'wee' followed by a low 'woo' – whilst whistling him, and refrain from experimentation or creative hubris.

In return for this, I would receive:

1. A personalised fuzzy wake-up service, involving the gentle tap-tapping of a paw on my cheek between the hours of 6.30 and 7 a.m. daily.
2. A plentiful supply of mice, with no obligation to eat the spleens thereof.
3. A proud, reassuring face in the window upon arriving home.
4. My first experience of the rare and spectacular 'feline vertical take-off'.
5. Truly remarkable displays of aptitude for the game of 'Lawn Green Voles' (aka 'Rodent Keepie-Uppies').
6. The knowledge that he would never be far from the end of my bed, particularly in times of trouble.

Owning Monty could perhaps best be described as a bit like owning an unusually intelligent, non-sycophantic dog that took care of its own faeces. And, like a dog, Monty enjoyed nothing more than the opportunity to stretch his legs at his owner's side. My first experience of this was one morning in 1990 when, having completed about half of my mile-long walk to the school bus stop, I turned to see him trotting happily behind me. Not really wishing to introduce him to Wayne Smith and Beau O'Dowd or the rest of first period double biology, I walked him back home, got a mini Crunchie out of the kitchen cupboard and pretended to get settled on the sofa, then made a run for it out the back door before he had chance to follow me.

My parents had moved to relative suburbia by then, so further exploring the much-overlooked pastime of man and mog rambling would have been impractical for all sorts of reasons, not least of them a Harvester, a motorway sliproad and a neighbouring estate regularly featured on the national news due to its collective love of pyromania. Still, I made a mental note to look further into the matter the next time we moved back to the country. Experience told me that it was only a matter of time before we did.

My parents moved house a lot during my childhood. For me, it was part of the rhythm of life. You went to a house, you began to meet some new friends, then, around a year later, your mum came into your bedroom with a sombre look on her face and told you it was once again time to pack up your ZX81 and your *Beano* annuals. By the time I was in my late teens and had moved to my seventh and final childhood home, I was starting to get a little sick of the upheaval, and the last thing I wanted was to live in a rented cottage in the north Nottinghamshire outback, eleven miles from the nearest gig venue, a mile down a country lane not wide enough to permit two cars to pass one another without one of them nosing into the hedgerow.

It was, however, a very good place to walk a cat.

There was no lead or choke chain involved, and Monty didn't take long to pick up the rules. If a car or a Border collie was coming in the other direction, you zipped into the undergrowth, leaving your adversary blinking in disbelief, writing off the small white blob they'd seen in the periphery of their vision as a trick of the light. You then walked along parallel to your owner on the field on the other side of the hedge until the coast was clear. Much of the time, though, Monty and I had only each other for company. Having been told to 'WATCH OUT FOR NUTTERS!' by my dad at the front door – my dad always told me to watch out for nutters, wherever I went, but in this part of north Nottinghamshire his concern was more justified than usual – we'd set off up the hill and do an entire circuit of the Forestry Commission land overlooking our house: a walk of around three miles, which lasted almost as long as the refreshing drink of water Monty took out of the toilet when we returned home.

A wearer of spiritual breeches, he always looked extremely noble on our walks, striding out in front of me. Every so often, feeling it was necessary to puncture this self-satisfied, dignified air, I would jog ahead of him and hide in a bush. This was a shameless exercise, carried out purely to get him to do something he felt very self-conscious about: meow. Monty's speaking voice was an incongruously high-pitched, effete thing, and he only used it when absolutely necessary. I fooled him every time: two minutes after making my lair in the foliage, he'd arrive, squeak-wailing with genuine terror that he had lost me for ever. Either that, or he was just humouring me. After all, what kind of bloke in his late teens would hide from his cat? You'd have to treat a simpleton like that kindly and patiently, wouldn't you?

Monty and I had eleven years together in total. During that time, we had just about as perfect a relationship as was possible between man and man cat – both of us ineradicably bonded, but always keeping a sensible, masculine distance. When I was feeling low or ill, Monty was there – not up for a cuddle, maybe, but offering strong silent support, a bit like Gary Cooper with whiskers. When Monty wanted to walk past his favourite hollow tree – it never had anything in the hollow bit, but he remained optimistic – he could count on me. He didn't fetch my paper or bark when I called him, but he knew which of the manifold noises I made meant 'I'm cooking with chicken and if you promise not to claw the carpet you can have some' and which one meant 'I'm putting some more of this horrendous ground-up slop in a dish – please get rid of it quickly.' Similarly, I knew which of his rare and perfect squeaks meant 'I have caught and methodically assassinated one of Sherwood Forest's many stoats' and which one meant 'I went into the downstairs loo for another drink out of the bowl and now the door has inconveniently swung shut behind me.'

When I moved out of home permanently in the summer of 1998, I agonised over whether to take Monty with me, but the two-bedroom terrace just outside Nottingham that my girlfriend and I had put a rental deposit on had only the smallest of gardens, backing onto a supermarket car park. It was no place to take a cat accustomed to strolling authoritatively around his own infinite green kingdom. Who knows? I reasoned. Maybe in time I'll have more space. I was right about that, but I didn't realise that it was time itself, not space, that was the issue.

I'd been gone only four weeks when my dad found his body. Monty looked as pristine as ever, lying in the dew-soaked grass, they said. Was it a heart attack that had killed him? Rat poison? An embolism? Nobody knew, and it did not occur to my mum to take Monty's body to the vet to find out. The way she saw it at the time, it would not have made any difference. Only later did she and my dad begin to concoct other theories: a vindictive milkman, some local yobs from Ockwold, the nearby village. My maternal grandfather – the man whom I was named after – had died of a brain haemorrhage at the age of forty-six, suddenly, after a life of near-perfect health, but it didn't occur to me that a similar thing could happen to a cat, least of all *this* cat. Monty's indefatigable constitution had been legendary, his nose cuts self-healing in seemingly a matter of hours, his flesh a thing that vets came to dread on vaccination day.

I'd been working in London on the day it happened, mobile phoneless, and by the time I received the call, my parents had buried him beneath a damson tree in the garden (a place he'd often liked to sit, in duck-style posture, casually sizing up some errant partridges from next door). When I arrived that evening, all that remained of his presence was a half-eaten bowl of biscuits.

As I slunk back to my car after the tears had dried up, I heard myself whistle him, which was strange, because I had not moved my mouth. I wheeled round, stunned and paranoid, until I remembered the bird that liked to sit on the telephone wire outside my bedroom, alternately mimicking the sound of our cordless telephone and that time-honoured 'wee-woo' that signalled it was time for Monty's dinner. I listened for a moment, with half a mind to curse such a wretched, heartless sky beast. But I had to concede that it had a point, and as I drove home to my catless house that 'wee-woo' ran on a loop on my internal jukebox. 'Wee-woo, wee-woo, wee-woo . . .' it went, until it finally mutated into a different song altogether, played to the same tune: 'Your fault, your fault, your fault . . .'

That night I made a vow: from that point on, I would live a catless life. I remember feeling pretty determined about it at the time. Looking back now, it was obvious I felt that I had reached a turning point in my life. I just didn't realise *which* turning point.

THE ONES THAT GOT AWAY: A LIST OF SOME CATS THAT I WOULDN'T HAVE MINDED OWNING BUT, OWING TO INSURMOUNTABLE OBSTACLES, COULDN'T

Bagpuss (1976–9)

Colour: New rave pink and white.

Home: Emily's shop (what kind of 7-year-old owns a shop?).

Owner: Emily.

Defining Features and Characteristics: Can't-be-bothered manner, all-round sagginess, propensity for hoarding junk and dreaming up improbable stories involving mermaids.

Catchphrase: 'Yeoooaaawnnnn!'

Why It Could Never Work between Us: Possessiveness of Emily could mutate into homicidal rage, upon finding favourite cloth possession gone. Limited need for old rags, bottles, shoes and assorted other old tat in my house.

Scampi (1988–93)

Colour: Tortoiseshell.

Home: Cripsley Edge Golf Club, Nottingham.

Owner: Club Steward, Cripsley Edge Golf Club.

Defining Features and Characteristics: Roly-poly yet stand-offish manner, unpredictable hiss valve, tendency to walk onto eighteenth green at inappropriate moments.

Catchphrase: 'It's not me, it's you.'

Why It Could Never Work between Us: Growing antipathy towards golf (mine), growing antipathy towards being over-stroked by Ladies Bridge Team leading to lasting grumpiness and 'I'm not just a plaything' hissy-fits (Scampi's).

Grundy (1994–8)

Colour: Ginger and white.

Home: Gedling, Nottingham.

Owners: Absentee couple at rear of girlfriend's house.

Defining Features and Characteristics: Nicotine-stained Rod Stewart meow. Take-me-home eyes.

Catchphrase: 'I am a cat of constant sorrow.'

Why It Could Never Work between Us: Constant low rasping noises very beguiling, but potentially grating on a day-to-day basis, not to mention possible hitch in any kidnap plot.

Archie (1995)

Colour: Deep tabby.

Home: York.

Owner: Unknown.

Defining Features and Characteristics: Waddling run, enormous belly, suspicious need to get into broom cupboards.

Catchphrase: 'Yeah, so I've got a boy's name – big deal. It never stopped Jamie Lee Curtis. What did you think I'm carrying in here – bananas?'

Why it Could Never Work between Us: My curtailed stay in locality because of dropping out of university after three months. Possible offspring rehoming problems.

Hercules (1996)

Colour: Rich Tea tabby.

Home: Newcastle-upon-Tyne.

Owner: Science Faculty of the University of Newcastle-upon-Tyne (unconfirmed).

Defining Features and Characteristics: Formidable bulk perfectly meshed with winning softness. Penchant for wrestling with undergraduates.

Catchphrase: 'Love the one you're with!'

Why It Could Never Work between Us: Limited visiting privileges. Insecurity deriving from unacademic status. Danger of squashage. Potential 'How can I know you truly love me, when you love everyone else too?' disagreements.

Nameless Strangely Silent Cat from Italian Campsite Where Feral Dogs Kept Me Awake at Night (1998)

Colour: Black.

Home: Donoratico, Tuscany.

Owner: Unknown.

Defining Features and Characteristics: Unaccountable fondness for getting under wheel arches, laconicism bordering on the disturbing.

Catchphrase: '. . .'

Why it Could Never Work Between us: Language barrier. Geographical obstacles which could only be conquered by Mediterranean move on my part and, even then, would probably lead to constant state of worry about attack from Tuscan wild dogs.

The Cat Man Cometh

If you decided to walk through suburbia with me in the early months of this century, you were always going to end up regretting it.

Ask Surreal Ed, my regular nightclubbing friend of the time. Ed and I did a lot of walking back then: keyed-up, aimless walking, hungover, euphoric walking. He would have told you all about the surprising dangers, particularly on a wet day, of that cypress bush on the road leading from Crouch Hill to Archway tube station. But Ed always gave as good as he got, and it wasn't like I was going to push just *anyone* into a cypress bush when they weren't expecting it. I would have had to have known you for at least two or three years first, and you would probably have been an Ed kind of person to get that kind of treatment (the kind of person, in short, who is apt to grab one of their friends' limbs in public at an entirely random moment, suffers from restless leg syndrome, and thinks the root of all great comic routines involves liberal use of the word 'cheese'). But even if you were a virtual stranger, not given to surrealism and safe from the maws of dripping shrubbery, you would soon have realised that, by taking a leisurely stroll with me through the leafy streets of north London, you had made a big mistake.

Everything would probably have started in companionable, sane enough fashion. Maybe you would have told me about a band or film you'd seen the previous night. 'Tom seems like a good listener!' you might have thought. 'He seems to be genuinely taking on board my view about the *Nutty Professor II* being slightly less funny than having a digit removed with a rusty hacksaw!' Perhaps we'd reached a higher level of intimacy in our relationship, and you were telling me about a person at work on whom you had a crush. You'd paced your story well, and you were just about to get to the long-delayed climax, where the steadfast but ultimately dull colleague of you and your prospective squeeze had unexpectedly had to depart early to catch a train, leaving just the two of you in the pub, alone for the first time ever. As you began to describe the powerful feelings of wanting – no, needing – to kiss someone, but not quite knowing if you should, you watched, somewhat disheartened, as my eyes began to glaze over and I darted across the street behind a wall. What, you wondered, could I possibly be doing? Thirty seconds later, when I emerged, no longer alone, you found out.

'Isn't he ace?' I would have said to you, holding my new friend's paws up for inspection. 'Have you ever seen such a cuddly fella?'

'Er, no,' you would have probably replied. 'He's . . . very nice. Do you think the owners will mind you doing that?'

'Oh, we're just making friends. Aren't we? *Aren't* we? I want to take *you* home. Oh yes, you like that now, don't you? Is that your favourite place? On your scruff?'

You are now starting to look at your watch. Somewhere in the adjacent house, a curtain twitches.

'How about a bit of chin-rubby action? Hmm? Is that nice? Oh yes, that's a very manly purr you've got, isn't it? If you were in the Mafia, you'd be the Mogfather, wouldn't you?'

You are edging away ever-so slightly now.

'I'm ever so sorry my lovely new meowy friend, but Tom has to go to the pub now. But he will come back and see you again. Yes, *he will*. You can be sure about that, because you're the best cat in the world. Yes, you are. You *are*.'

I should probably point out here that this is no 'I was young and slightly deranged, but it's all better now' recollection; to this day, I still find it hard to walk along a road without befriending every cat in the vicinity, but it could definitely be said that, in the period surrounding my twenty-fifth birthday, that same befriending had taken on a somewhat more . . . rabid . . . quality than usual. In fact, many of my friends from that time would argue that 'befriending' was not quite the right word. 'Marrying' might have been more appropriate.

'You *really* like cats, don't you?'

What can I say? When you've taken a wrong turn into a cat-free life style, you have to get your moggy-loving where you can, even if that moggy-loving happens to be on the run.

It had been two years since Monty's death and, in that time, I'd reached an acceptance of sorts: if not an acceptance that there was anything predestined or inescapable about his death, then at least an acceptance that, put in the same position again, without the benefit of being fore-warned, I probably would still have chosen not to take him with me to my new home. Nonetheless, I could not shake my certainty that the slightest nudge of a butterfly's wings on my part – a slightly longer walk together, one more bit of chicken – could have kept him from his fate in that cold wet grass. Having taken my deserter's shame and vowed to spend my time in cat-free limbo, I'd been pretty disciplined about it. Although how 'disciplined' I would have been had I not relocated, a few months later, to a gardenless flat in London is hard to say.

My move south had been necessitated by a new job: I'd been made Rock Critic of the *Guardian* newspaper. Living in the sticks might not seem the ideal preparation for a job writing about pop music, but my boondocks homelife in my late teens and early twenties had given me the time and space to learn my craft quickly, making up for the cultural years I'd lost as a teenager by pursuing my dream of becoming a golf professional.

That house on the outskirts of the village of Ockwold in north Nottinghamshire, outside which Monty had died, might not have provided a music-mad twenty-something's ideal choice of lifestyle, but it had been the place where I'd turned myself round from a two-time college dropout, bouncing between income support and jobs in factories and supermarkets, to a music writer for a national newspaper. It was here that I'd corresponded with musicians in Denver, Colorado, and Athens, Georgia, and written and edited the cheaply produced fanzine that had secured me a job writing for the *New Musical Express*. The well-spoken, largely druggy, largely public-schooled men who commissioned me to write about American art rockers and the ageing hipsters of sixties and seventies pop had no idea that I did so at a desk facing a field full of cows, three miles away from the nearest bus stop and eleven from the nearest gig venue, just as they had no idea that I'd failed four of my GCSEs and lasted under three months as a BA Honours student. This was not down to subterfuge on my part: in the music journo world, talking about your background was uncool and bourgeois, and it was obvious that most of my peers saw any place beyond London's North Circular that wasn't Manchester, Liverpool or Glasgow as an irrelevance, and certainly not something that would merit the interruption of a dissection of the latest Rocket From The Crypt single.

Once I visited the pub next to the *NME* office with some of the staff, and one of them put a question to the table regarding where everyone had been when they first heard Love's classic *Forever Changes* album. As achingly credible answer ('getting head in a goth girl's flat') followed achingly credible answer ('getting stoned by the Thames and watching the sun come up'), I became increasingly uncertain as I thought about my own response ('sitting in my bedroom, clearing up shrew blood and trying to get a plague of harvest midges off my pillow'), and was relieved when the subject changed before I had a chance to voice it. I was not ashamed of my bumpkin status – in fact, without really knowing it, I probably quite liked the way it set me apart – but I realised that it was time to get a little closer to the action.

For more than a year, I'd thrown myself more or less as boisterously into London life as was possible without actually scaling Big Ben and doing the caterpillar on its roof. Like a lot of other music journalists I knew, I drank lots and lots of beer and went to four or five gigs every week. Unlike a lot of music journalists I knew, I invariably celebrated the end of those gigs by going to a nightclub and dancing my socks off to the funk and disco hits of the distant past, then – if there was an extra half an hour or more to be wrung out of the night – another nightclub, where I would do the same thing all over again. It was not a life that invited pet ownership, but I'd enjoyed it thoroughly. It was, however, always going to be little more than an interlude. If I had not rushed off in the direction of the RSPCA or the Cats Protection League in the aftermath of Monty's death, I may have told myself it was because I was keeping my vow, but, more likely, it was because I secretly worried about the extreme acts of feline philanthropy that might ensue. I'd always loved cats: their fuck-you swagger, the art of their paws and tails and muzzles, the ageless comedy of their innate touchiness, the way they made every smidgen of affection they gave you feel like a hard-won personal victory. But now my lifelong need to be in their good books had the fuel injection of guilt. If I could not have all the cats, it seemed easier to have none.

Well, 'none' is not strictly true. I did actually have *one* cat. Sort of.

Daisy had never been intended for me in the first place, and while the official line was that she was my mum's, it would be inaccurate to say that she was spiritually owned by anyone. A scraggy bundle of fully formed tortoiseshell neuroses, she'd appeared under our kitchen table one day in 1991, a present from my cousin Fay, whose friend's cat had recently had a litter. Caught off guard, we were nevertheless pleased to welcome Daisy into our family, although Daisy's feelings on her new domestic set-up were more ambivalent. They became more ambivalent still after being chased under the bed by Monty.

Human nicknames are so often glibly explained, but cat nicknames tend to evolve in a more visceral, abstract manner. Why did I sometimes call Monty 'The Ponce'? It's hard to say. One day, for a reason known only to herself (if that), my mum decided to call him 'Ponsonby'. I shortened this, adding the 'The', possibly to acknowledge some aura

of aristocracy. Daisy's transformation into 'The Slink', however, was less of a mystery. You wouldn't exactly have called
what Monty did to Daisy bullying; his regular chasing and
rugby-tackling of her never involved flying fur, and seemed
to be just his casual way of reminding her that he quite
simply didn't have time in his impeccably managed feline
schedule for a shilly-shallying neurotic step-sister – let
alone one with the bizarre defect of hissing when she was
happy and purring when she was agitated. With each subsequent attack, her posture, which had been somewhat
sausage dog-ish in the first place, became more low-slung,
until it was clear that by continuing to call her by her original moniker we would have been lying to her and to
ourselves.

Since Monty's death, The Slink had not exactly come
out of her shell in the manner we'd expected – though no
doubt my dad, reminded on a daily basis of the loss of the
beloved, solid Monty by The Slink's sheer nervy unMonty-
ness, did not help with his stomping feet and foghorn shouts
of 'OY!' every time she strayed towards his favourite armchair. I knew I had not put the effort into my relationship
with The Slink that I needed to, and our contact had
petered out into a series of pessimistically proffered hands,
sudden shooting movements under sofas and strangely irate
purring sessions.

I told myself I was content with this for a while: I had a
lively social life, a good job, and a cat – albeit a possibly
mentally disturbed one that barely seemed to remember
who I was – that I could go and see every month or two. But
in summer 2000, when I moved from Crouch End (borders)
in north London to the leafier Blackheath (borders) in
south London, began to lay off the beer, get a little more
sleep and spend a little more time at home, I realised that all

I had been doing was keeping my love of cats in an under-sized suitcase: I could press down on its lid, but it would spring open sooner or later with renewed vigour.

When the contents of the suitcase began their inevitable spill, it must have proved disturbing for the hard-living, bohemian men with whom I spent most of my time in those days – men who'd probably presumed that my first love was Budweiser or Fleetwood Mac – not to mention for sportier, animal-indifferent longer-term acquaintances like Surreal Ed, who'd never had cause to cross paths with my cat side before. As a 25-year-old, I could count my cat-mad male pals on the fingers of one finger.[1] We might have been entering a brave new male millennium, containing such unthinkably evolved phenomena as hair serum, exfoliating face scrub and George Clooney, but for the longer-haired men working in or around the notoriously androgynous sphere of music, to witness the bonding process between man and cat could still apparently be a scary thing. I can see that it must have been odd to be walking along having a perfectly normal conversation with someone who you'd pegged as having fairly simple priorities in life, and then see him suddenly cross the street in the direction of a ball of fur and begin acting like his brain has been transplanted with that of a self-neglecting 72-year-old widow. But what was the big deal? The way I viewed it, there were lots of very

[1] Leo was terrific, one of the most fun-loving friends you could hope for. He also had one of the droopiest moustaches in north London and liked nothing better than a Saturday spent vicariously clothes shopping with his best female friends. Those girls who guessed wrongly at his sexual orientation didn't know the hours of fun they were missing – not just in the vintage section of Top Shop, but in his flat, with his ageing tabby, Tab-Tab, a cat so docile it would gaze up lovingly at Leo as he used its plush back fur to polish the parquet floor of his Kentish Town flat.

ugly things in London, so, on the occasions when something beautiful with a glossy coat came along and nudged
its cold nose into your hand, it seemed churlish not to take
a few moments to celebrate the mere fact of its existence.

The situation, strangely, was little better with the opposite sex. One might have thought that expressing an interest
in finding a female partner who loved cats was the male
equivalent of a woman saying, 'I've always wanted to go out
with a bloke who loved football and farting.' Nonetheless,
up to this point, all the girls I'd fallen for had either been
indifferent or allergic to my favourite animals. The eyes of
my last girlfriend had been apt to puff up at the mere mention of the words 'Radcliffe on Trent RSPCA' and while
we'd managed to pretend a cat-free existence was working
for a while in our Nottingham terrace, it became obvious
our set-up was doomed when I began trying to win the affections of next door's big-nosed black and white tom, Charlie,
with a selection of cooked meats from the delicatessen at
the nearby Co-op. You know you're starved of feline affection when you're in a noise pollution dispute with people
and you still can't stop yourself from feeding kabanos to
their moggy. I imagine the two girls who endlessly blasted
Stardust's 'Music Sounds Better with you' through our partition wall must have muttered to their *Sun*-reading
boyfriends about 'the weird bloke next door' who was so
mysteriously fond of the cat that appeared to hold so little
appeal for them (or significantly less appeal than Phats and
Small's 'Turn Around', anyway).

Dee could not have been more different.

I'm sure I'd already worked out that she was the girl for
me prior to that September night when we went on that
seemingly endless yet effortless walk through south London,
but the encounter with the ginger bruiser really sealed the

deal. I forget exactly what street in Blackheath we were strolling along at the time, but I still remember the feeling of acceptance when I picked him up and Dee neither fidgeted nor put her hands on her hips, but began to join me in praising his hirsute majesty.

For a year, I had seen Dee at parties, at gigs, in offices: we seemed to go to all the same places, and know a lot of the same people, but always missed getting introduced by a matter of minutes. When we finally met, the bond was instant. That Dee was the most intelligent, funny and beautiful girl I'd ever met knocked me off my feet; that she liked many of the same films, books and albums as me was a bonus; that she was a cat lover too was almost too good to be true. Better still, she had two of her own.

'They hate me, though,' she said, as she began to work her fingers through Big Ginge's scruff. 'One of them, especially. He's an evil genius. I only have to look at him, and I know he's plotting my downfall.'

I found this extremely hard to believe, particularly looking at Big Ginge, who, if he got more putty-like in her hands, could probably quite easily have been talked into a game of 'Fetch!' on one of south London's numerous commons. Dee was clearly exaggerating. As a stalwart of cat ownership, I knew how easy it was to feel that a feline was giving you the cold shoulder. Living with a cat was sometimes a bit like being at a media party and talking to an unusually carnivorous F-list celebrity: the kind whose eyes never left you in any doubt that they'd dump you in the blink of an eye for a tasty canapé or a former cast member of a daytime soap opera. The disdainful looks, the hot and cold moods, the 'talk to the tail' gestures . . . you got hardened to all this after a while. And while I didn't like to boast, I felt that Dee's problems would soon come to an end, once my magic touch was introduced to the equation. After all, it wasn't just anyone who could walk down a street in Blackheath and coax thirty-pound furry ginger ruffians to sit on their shoulder and purr. That sort of thing took a rare combination of animal cunning, patience, studied nonchalance and intuition – qualities that I had worked hard on attaining, while in the company of my cats, and countless more belonging to a mixture of relatives, friends, enemies and indifferent strangers.

Nonetheless, Dee was insistent and, as we began to spend more time together, her reports of the betrayals of her eldest cat, The Bear, become increasingly extreme.

The Bear's story was an unremittingly traumatic one, beginning in a plastic bag on the hard shoulder of the M23, where he was found, huddled together with six of his brothers and sisters, by a south-east London pet shop owner. Upon getting him home for the first time, Dee had watched, impotently, while his tiny, coiled black form had made three unsuccessful attempts to run through a closed window, finally sliding down it and retreating to a scowling position behind the sofa, where he would stay for the next fourteen hours. Overlooking one grudgingly proffered ear for a tickle (The Bear's, not Dee's), the first sign of affection did not come until a week or so later, although Dee was somewhat surprised to find it aimed not at her, but at her friend Neil, a kohl-eyed singer in a gothic rock outfit whose pastimes included tracing inscriptions from gravestones and locking himself in his room to compose poetry on a 1950s manual typewriter.

'I think from that point on, I started to realise something about his taste in men,' she explained. Fortunately, as she was the bassist in an artsy garage rock band at this point, Dee tended to fraternise with a fair few males of intense disposition. It was these artistic men who were on the receiving end of The Bear's infrequent yet frighteningly zealous padding and wrist-nipping sessions, but it was Dee who was left to clear up his violently scattered cat litter and gently bathe the hole torn in his throat by an East End alleycat.

The Bear had a way of looking at you, Dee said, that made you feel directly responsible for his hardship. This look only grew more intense after Dee, her actor boyfriend of the time and The Bear had contracted carbon monoxide poisoning in their east London flat. After a trip to hospital, Dee and The Actor soon recovered, but the effects on The Bear were more permanent. Asthma could be added to a list of ailments that already included a permanently perforated neck, a winky eye, a torn ear, a sight defect, a crooked tail and an inferiority complex roughly the size of Wales. He also now had the fluffy, frustatingly lowbrow presence of Dee's new kitten, Janet, to deal with.

The beginning of 2000 had seen a rare mellow period for The Bear. Not only had he begun to break down The Actor's lifelong antipathy towards cats and form a strong, moody bond with him, he had also, for the first time in his life, managed to go four months without a visit to the vets. Dee and The Actor's split that summer, however, had changed all that. The subsequent house move and the accompanying separation from The Actor would have been stressful enough for The Bear, even if it had not coincided with him developing a new flea allergy that made all his hair fall out. The fact that the treatment for the flea allergy *also* made his hair fall out seemed to have silenced any doubts that The Bear had had about Dee being anything other than his ultimate foe. From that point on, it had been full-scale warfare. Or, at least, the kind of full-scale warfare in which one army uses all the physical and psychological weaponry at their disposal while the other army cowers in the trenches, periodically offering their tormentors over-priced parma ham and attempting to boost their fragile self-esteem with comments like, 'You're beautiful – people don't always see it, but you really are.'

Dee had finally found a course of flea treatment for The Bear that was slowly restoring his fur, but, the week before I made my first visit to her flat, he'd begun to shed, bafflingly, furiously, once again. Now gardenless, he had also decided that the litter tray – seemingly permanently full with Janet's titanic cargo, no matter how frequently Dee emptied it – was the domain of a more uncouth, less intellectually tortured kind of cat. It's always a bit of a shock when, thirty seconds after setting foot in your new partner's home for the first time, you're confronted with excrement, but any squeamish feelings I had about coming face to face with my first Bear turd were stifled by my fascination regarding just how he'd squeezed it into the pocket of Dee's freshly laundered dressing gown. 'He must have . . . squatted sideways,' I said, evaluating the evidence.

'Oh, that's nothing,' said Dee, reaching for a wet wipe and a swing bin liner. 'Put it this way – if I were you, I wouldn't leave your wallet hanging about while you're here.'

Two hours later, the perpetrator still had not emerged. 'Do you think he's escaped?' I asked Dee.

'No. How could he? The windows are all locked. He's around here somewhere. I can feel his gaze. He's probably looking at us disapprovingly right now and we don't even know it.'

Dee's flat only had one bedroom and a living room barely big enough to gently rock a cat in, let alone to swing a very nervous one, but four years of studiously dodging mankind meant The Bear was well schooled in the art of camouflage. The same could not be said for Janet, who, moments after we had entered the flat and found the soiled dressing gown, had bounded into the living room like an overenthusiastic Labrador and very narrowly avoided trampling the crime scene with devastating results. I found this great galumphing creature hard to reconcile with the small black furball Dee had described as being brought to her door by two East End urchins, one Dickensian-sounding night the previous winter.

'Our dad's died, miss, and we were wondering if you wanted our cat,' the children had pleaded. Since a) Janet was being held upside down by one of the urchins, and it looked like one of her appendages might fall off if she was suspended there for much longer and b) a crucial episode of *Friends* was on TV at the time, Dee made a snap decision, accepted the challenge, and whisked Janet into her life, where she had resided in a state of vacant happiness ever since – the one minor upset being the moment when Dee took her to the vets to be spayed, only to find out that she'd been misinformed regarding 'her' gender.[2]

By the time we'd been to collect an Indian takeaway and got settled on the sofa with Janet sprawled at our feet (my magic touch had worked: as soon as I'd started tickling him on the side of his head, he'd melted into the cushion next to me), I'd almost forgotten about The Bear. I'd expected that, if he was going to emerge from his hiding place, it would be a gradual process: a tentative nose poked out from behind a cupboard or wardrobe, a nervous paw, a step back, a step forward, a suspiciously twitching nostril. It

---

[2] 'How was I to know?' protested Dee. 'It's very fluffy down there.'

was more than a bit of a surprise to turn my gaze away from the TV and see him no more than two inches from my chicken bhuna, sitting pertly upright and staring straight into my eyes.

'Aha,' said Dee. 'That's something I forgot to tell you. The Bear *loves* Indian food.'

I'd heard so much about him for so long now that it came as a little bit of a shock to find that he was, after all this, only a cat. I'd been half-expecting some sort of cross between Gollum and the suicidal kid from *Dead Poet's Society*. What I saw looked more like a Tasmanian devil. In fact, it looked like two Tasmanian devils melded together: the crazed, big-headed, skinny-limbed sort from the *Looney Tunes* cartoons, and the somewhat more ursine real-life model. His face was round and Paddington-like, and went a certain way to justifying his moniker, but the forlorn, balding pipecleaner body that slunk behind it was anything but bearlike. I'd seen piglets with thicker pelts on them. Only his tail, still but crooked at a slightly inquisitive angle, seemed to speak of any kind of vitality.

'I know. It's awful, isn't it? Whenever he meets a new person, I always feel terrible,' said Dee. 'I ask myself, "Am I a bad owner?" But I really have tried to make his life easier. When you're taking home £150 a month after rent, it's not easy paying that many vet's bills. He's just a cat who seems to find trouble wherever he goes.'

It's said that, in terms of cat communication, there is nothing ruder than a wide-eyed stare. If you want to make friends with a cat, you must squint gently in their direction to demonstrate that you mean them no harm, or look away from them altogether. I'd never been so sure about this: one of the rare and special things about Monty had been that he'd frequently looked directly into my eyes, bolstering my belief that he saw me as a living, breathing friend and not just a subservient actor in the solipsistic film of his life. Nonetheless, Monty had never looked at me like *this*. A lifetime of pain seemed to swim around in The Bear's soulful peepers. I also couldn't shake the feeling that, on the other side of them, a screen was currently spooling personal data, Terminator-style.

NAME: TOM

AGE: 25

HEIGHT: FIVE FEET ELEVEN AND
THREE-QUARTERS.

FEELING ABOUT NEVER HAVING QUITE
GOT TO SIX FOOT: MILDLY RESENTFUL
BORDERING ON BITTER.

NUMBER OF PREVIOUS CATS: FOUR (FIVE
IF YOU COUNT THE ONE THAT USED TO LIVE
TWO DOORS AWAY FROM HIS NAN, WHICH HE
PRETENDED WAS HIS WHEN ITS OWNERS
WERE OUT AT WORK).

LIKES: ANIMALS, HAIRY SEVENTIES
ROCK MUSIC, FIZZY SWEETS.

HEROES: KRAMER FROM SEINFELD,
THE DUDE FROM THE BIG LEBOWSKI.

SPECIAL TALENTS: GOLF CLUB KEEPIE-
UPPIES, DISCO DANCING, HAVING A 'KNACK'
WITH CATS (HE RECKONS).

WEAK AREAS: CUTE WHISKERS, COLD NOSES,
BIG BESEECHING GREEN EYES, CLOTHING.

PROPENSITY FOR FELINE SOPPINESS: 9.8/10.

POTENTIAL AS HUMAN PAWN IN
GAME OF CAT LIFE: 9.9/10.

A few weeks previously, I'd written a negative review
of a rather tedious, recalcitrant country rock album for a
national newspaper. The day it had been printed had been
a Friday, so, what with that being one of the seven days
of the week, that night I'd been to a nightclub. Towards
closing time, a man whom I vaguely knew from the record
company that had released the album, whom I was aware
to be unhappy with the review, had approached me and
said, 'Come on! We can't just keep having this stand-off
all night. I suppose we should put this behind us.' Until
that moment, I hadn't known the man was even *at* the
nightclub, never mind that he had spent much of the night
shooting metaphorical daggers at me. I was also confused
at just what we needed to put behind 'us', when all I had
done was been a bit sarcastic about a record made by some
despondent men in Stetsons.

The Bear's unflinching gaze was similarly disturbing and
flummoxing. What had I done to him to merit such a
piercing look? Had I unwittingly snubbed him in the street
for a well-manicured tabby at some point several months
before? Maybe he'd helped release a depressive country
record, too; from what I knew of his résumé so far, it didn't
seem beyond the bounds of possibility. There was always
the additional chance that this was all about jealousy. I
failed to see the logic, if you were worried about the wandering eye of a loved one, in planting a large piece of
excrement in that same loved one's nightwear. Then
again, nobody ever claimed the affairs of the heart were
straightforward.

We'd probably been looking at each other for forty-five
seconds now, though it felt more like forty-five minutes. It
was the kind of staring contest that tends to be broken only
by a passionate embrace, a crying jag or someone getting the

crap beaten out of them. I felt that the first option was unlikely, though I couldn't entirely rule out the last two.

One of us had to break the deadlock, and it was pretty clear it wasn't going to be him. 'Um . . . The *Bear*!' I called, in my friendliest singsong voice, glancing nervously across to Dee. I was used to calling out preposterous cat names in a camp voice, but this felt somehow wrong: like Eva Braun getting Hitler in for his dinner by cheerfully shouting, 'The *Führer*!'

He took a nervous step forward, his eyes never leaving mine, and sniffed a chunk of my chicken bhuna. I'd actually been saving that particular bit for later, to wrap in some nan bread, but I figured I could let it go, just this once. He took a lick, then another lick, then heard something utterly terrifying at a frequency undetectable to the human ear, jolted into an alert, upright pose, gave me one last look of disgust and scarpered in the direction of some boxes. It would be the last we saw of him that evening.

'It could have been worse,' said Dee. 'At least he didn't puke in your trainers. I actually think he quite likes you.'

The following morning, I woke to find the sun beaming through my tiny studio flat in Blackheath. Returning from a morning stroll across the heath to get a newspaper, I could not help but bask in the goodly shine of the universe. Normally, when I felt energised like this, I would already have been looking forward to my first beer of that evening, but now my mind was not on the pub, or that night's gig. In all that time I'd been burning the midnight oil had I just been trying to light the way to the right cat-loving girl? It seemed so. As I moved towards my desk, even the knowledge that I had to review the new Simply Red album later that day could not dampen my spirits. I noticed the green light blinking on my answerphone.

The message was from Dee. She did not exactly sound upset, but her tone had more of a quaver to it than usual. 'Don't take this personally, because I'm trying not to,' she said, 'but this morning The Bear got through the window and escaped. I've been all over looking for him, but he's gone.'

PUSS, MOG OR SUPERVILLAIN: SOME TELL-TALE (THOUGH NOT CONCLUSIVE) SIGNS TO LOOK OUT FOR WHEN TRYING TO WORK OUT THE BREED OF A NON-PEDIGREE CAT

Puss

- Propensity towards leanness.
- Chatty manner, which in more extreme cases results in 'office joker' reputation.
- Short hair.
- Expressive whiskers.
- Predilection for stretched sleeping positions.
- Fondness for window sitting.

Mog

- Greater tendency for success in the public eye.
- Sun-loving.
- Deep meow.
- Intrinsic sense of entitlement combined with 'won't get out of bed for less than £3,000' laziness.
- Longish-to-long hair.
- Predilection for huddled sleeping positions.
- Fondness for boxes.

Supervillain

- Unerring talent for camouflage and self-sufficient hiding spots.
- Unflinching eye contact.
- Resourceful bowel movements.
- Sensitive skin.
- Litany of long-standing grudges.
- Penchant for tightly scrunched sleeping positions.
- Constant need to be at higher-than-thou vantage points.

Beneath the Undermog

Thankfully The Bear didn't stay away for long – not that time, anyway. Because the flat had small opaque windows and backed onto an inaccessible area of waste land, it had been difficult for Dee to look for him, but she took the pragmatic view that a cat who could shin six feet up a wall and insinuate himself through a three-inch gap in a window could quite easily perform the reverse of the same feat. Sure enough, three days later, a wounded 'meyoeeyee' noise accompanied by the scrabble of claws on brick heralded his return – a return he chose to celebrate late that night in his own special way, deep in the enveloping comfort of a vintage handbag, bringing a whole new meaning to the phrase 'the wee hours'.

Dee, however, had seen that the writing was on the wall, and a few weeks later, she reluctantly handed him over to The Actor. Painful as this was for Dee, she had to face up to the logic of the situation, since The Actor had a) been missing The Bear hugely, b) lived in a flat with a garden and c) didn't own vintage handbags.

Over the following weeks, reports would filter back to us

of a completely different cat: a happy, frolicking bundle of quickly regrowing fur who could be seen skipping off over the fence of an evening, tail pertly in the air, to see if The Actor's neighbour's cat was 'coming out to play'.

'They even bite each other sometimes, apparently,' said Dee.

'How do you mean?' I asked.

'Oh, he gives The Bear a little nip on the neck, and The Bear nips him back on the forearm. Bit weird if you ask me, but at least they're getting on.'

Weird? It sounded *great*.

On one hand, I found myself viewing all this as a kind of defeat: I wasn't accustomed to cats disliking me and the fact that this one had belonged to the person with whom I was starting to think about spending the rest of my life, not to mention that I had been seemingly outcatted by a hardened mogophobe, made the failure sting all the more. On the other hand, I could not say I was totally unhappy with the situation. In the brief time I'd spent with The Bear, I had felt a little like an unwanted step-father trying to appease the problem child of his new spouse. Looking into his eyes, I had not been able to shake the feeling that he was up to something clandestine. He always had that air of someone *gathering data*.

And, after all, I'd got the cat I'd been hankering after, hadn't I? In February, Dee and I moved into an airy flat on the other side of Blackheath (borders), and I quickly began to cement my bond with Janet, although it's unlikely that this was anything to do with my natural cat aptitude, since bonding with Janet could hardly be considered a unique achievement. His circle of acquaintances included everyone from the postman, against whom he rubbed every morning, to the mangy fox with whom he regularly sat in sociable,

idiotic silence in the garden we shared with the two flats
below us. At one point, when I was sitting on the lawn with
him, he did find a vole, and I thought I was about to see his
long-suppressed dark side, but he just purred at it. His sole
enemy was a neighbouring muscular white and black tom,
with whom he could be found below our bedroom window
in the early hours engaged in another round of a marathon,
Beano-style punch-up: all clouds of smoke and random jut-
ting limbs.

As for The Bear, Janet had always liked him too. Seeing
them together, I had been reminded of John Steinbeck's *Of
Mice and Men*, with Janet as the big, dumb Lennie and The
Bear as the diminutive, scheming George. The only difference, perhaps, was that while Lennie was always an intrinsic
part of George's schemes, The Bear wouldn't usually have
lowered himself to include a nincompoop like Janet in his.
Most of the time, they'd found a way to peacefully co-exist
without anyone getting hissed at or sat upon, but just occasionally, Janet would feel an uncontrollable surge of
affection and rush out of nowhere towards his smaller companion, swamping him with his limbs. This would
invariably end with The Bear in an ungainly and unfeline
position, looking like a Mini Metro caught beneath the
undercarriage of a juggernaut.

He must have thought he'd finally rid himself of the big
populist retard when he moved to The Actor's flat, so I can
imagine his disappointment when, the following May, he
was forced into a convenient reunion. Dee had received a
call from The Actor explaining that he was in hospital
having been set upon by a gang of youths in Woolwich and
would be spending some time in recovery at his parents'
house. During this period, The Bear would once again come
into Dee's custody. Arrangements for the switchover quickly

ensued, the goods swapping hands on a dark street in neutral
territory, as if they were not a scrawny domestic cat but a
suitcase full of heroin or illegally imported panda claws.
After this, The Bear was transported to our living room,
where he edged out of his basket and sniffed the air nervously, before an excited Janet greeted him by squatting on
his spine.

In the six months since I'd last seen him, The Bear had put
on a few pounds. The fur on his back had resprouted, but his
stomach was still bald, and his face remained unusually
expressive and nuanced. That his expressions only seemed
to stretch from 'Wounded composer of verse' to 'Why the
fuck have you done this to me, you shitbat?' did not make
them any less remarkable in their soulful multitudes. He
clearly bore a grudge and, since I worked from home, I was
the one who tended to be on the receiving end of it most of
the time.

I've always felt that a house without a cat is a house without soul. Admittedly, it's often a *clean* house without soul,
but, as much as I hadn't missed the muddy paw prints and
discarded mouse stomachs in my cat hiatus of 1998–2000,
the places I'd lived had seemed sorely underpopulated and
hollow without the presence of a wet nose and a rubby tail;
like unusually cluttered show homes. In those years I'd fan-
tasised about a home office where self-loving lumps of fur
would drape themselves lazily over fax machines and key-
boards, and, since living with Janet, I'd been doing my best
to live the dream, postponing deadlines in order to stage
games of cat football against him in the living room using a
hacky-sack and attempting to train him to warm my feet
while I wrote. When one day he cut off an important

conversation I was having with an editor by flopping on the receiver, I couldn't bring myself to be mad, so pleased was I to have the chance to call back and say, 'Sorry about that: my cat just sat on the phone!' Less than a year before, this had been a scene from one of my ultimate daydreams: the stuff of wild, unattainable fantasy.

With the arrival of The Bear, however, this greeting card picture of Man and Cat harmony was strategically shattered. One of the problems was that, while Janet was now permitted to roam outdoors, his wandering, unpredictable step-brother could not be permitted, on any account, to follow him. 'Whatever you do, don't let him escape!' Dee would say, as she left for work in the morning. From there, a typical day would proceed with me returning from dropping her off at the train station and getting into a panic at finding a flat containing only one cat, then spending the next twenty minutes frantically looking for The Bear, before getting into a horizontal position on the kitchen floor and peering through a hole in the kickboard beneath the oven. Here I would find three eyes glinting back at me suspiciously. Paranoia and terror would take hold, as I speculated on exactly what kind of beast I was facing, until I realised that one of the eyes was just an old marble. Having managed to squeeze himself into the one corner unreachable to human hand by a matter of millimetres, The Bear would resist all attempts at bribery, meat-themed or otherwise, until, at about 10 a.m., I finally gave up and decided to get down to some work. For the next half an hour, all would be peaceful, until, in the corner of my vision, I'd see a streak of black smoke waft past my study door, pursued by a considerably more corpulent streak of black smoke with a lolling, enthusiastic tongue.

Janet might have been The Bear's tormentor, but in

truth, The Bear probably saw him as more of a nemesis than an enemy, and one of the things that made nemeses different from enemies was that you could sometimes put aside your differences and join forces with them. In many ways, it seemed that the pair were suddenly united in the goal of stopping me from getting anything vaguely productive done. Sometimes, I'd be disturbed at my desk by a hollow scraping sound from the next room, and arrive in the kitchen to find them both on their hind legs, tapping at cupboard doors like joint-casing diamond thieves or property surveyors testing partition walls.

What were they planning? And why was it that The Bear was able to time his asthmatic fits so perfectly with Janet's vomiting fits or industrial digging sessions in the litter tray? Had George decided that he could use Lennie to his advantage after all? And did Lennie even realise that he was part of the plan, or was he just really glad to have a playmate that wasn't an arthritic, senile fox?

Take pets of shin-height or above and use their unruliness as an excuse for your lack of productivity and you might get a certain amount of sympathy. Everyone's heard of 'problem dogs'. I imagine a volatile llama could be an absolute bugger when you're on deadline and were I to, say, invent a high-spirited ferret called Charles, the condolences would undoubtedly have flooded in. But cats are supposed to be background pets. Try explaining to a new parent that your cats are keeping you up at night and wait for the ensuing silence and subsequent unreturned phone calls. Nonetheless, please believe me when I say that those were tough days. Compared to the nights sandwiched between them, however, they were a picnic: an upbeat Barry Manilow-soundtracked scene from the feline remake of *Turner and Hooch*.

The Bear would usually wait until Dee and I were at our most tired before striking. Crawling into bed after a long day, feeling a little like arctic explorers in the final few moments before planting the flag, we would notice the stain, but usually not quickly enough not to be lying in it. Even in a near-comatose state, you'd find yourself taking time to admire the accuracy: if The Bear had used a tape measure and a compass, he could not have made his aim more central. On most occasions, even if we'd huddled next to the wall and held our stomachs in, we would have found it hard to avoid direct contact with the fruits of his labour.

There's a photograph taken by Dee that speaks volumes about this period of our lives. It shows me sitting under the duvet on the fold-out sofa bed on the living room, bleary and baggy-eyed. On either side of my feet sit Janet and The Bear, the former apparently happily preoccupied with some hamster-on-a-wheel footage on repeat play in his head, the latter staring demonically at the camera. On the back of the photo, Dee has scrawled 'Tom, Janet and The Bear: Blackheath, 2001 – on sofa bed because of The Bear'. Obviously, to any sane person, who has never been pushed around by a pet, there must seem something desperately wrong with this scene, and I have to admit that even I sometimes look at it and wonder at the wisdom of allowing your cats to take pride of place on your one remaining unsoiled bit of bedding five minutes after one of those cats has just weed on your mattress, but I know that by that point, normal human–cat etiquette could not be applied to the situation. The Bear had rocked my smug sense of cat veteran's wisdom. I was off balance. It wasn't just the strange 'meeo*op*' noises he would make in the middle of the night that would have me stumbling across to the kitchen to check if the battery in our smoke alarm needed replacing. Neither was it the nervous wait for the next suspicious brown stain or pool of liquid (you know you've got a problem pet when you find yourself pouring a cup of Earl Grey and asking yourself, 'Is it just me or does this taste slightly . . . tart?').

No, it would have been much more simple if I'd felt that The Bear plain didn't like me. What really made me uncertain were the intense displays of affection with which he seasoned his domestic terrorism. The Bear's rage scared me, but isn't it always actually the way with supervillains that they're at their most terrifying when they're being friendly? The Bear's fur was stubbly and porcupine-like when he was feeling misanthropic, but when he was in one of his spasmodic good moods it was as adhesive as Velcro. With him purring deeply and chillingly in my arms, I would feel as if he was trying to cleave himself to me permanently: it reminded me not so much of an overclingy girlfriend, more of a needy male friend whom you suspect, with a bit of encouragement, could start carving your name into his forearm.

These bouts of passion might have seemed spasmodic and irrational, but on closer inspection, they had a pattern. The Bear was always at his clingiest when I was feeling a bit under the weather, when Dee and I had exchanged testy words, or when I was nervously close to deadline with a piece of work.

I'd enjoyed writing about music for a living for the last seven years, but, almost as soon as I'd begun to be paid well for it, I'd began to get a lot more interested in writing itself, in the broader sense, than in being a breathlessly trend-conscious part of the music universe. I still got a lot of pleasure out of music, but I wanted to carry on getting a lot of pleasure out of it, and the way to do that, it seemed, was not to be a full-time music critic, so when the man from the glossy magazine with the big circulation called and asked if I'd like to write a guest slot in a regular column about domestic life, I immediately said yes.

'It's quite last minute, though,' he warned. 'We'd need you to make a decision in the next couple of hours. Something quirky about your day-to-day existence. The trivial stuff that runs through our brains and we often don't talk about. Any ideas?'

'Well there is something,' I said. 'It's a bit of an odd one.'

'Oh yes?'

'Well . . . it's just: I'm starting to think my cat is my girl-friend's ex-boyfriend in disguise.'

In retrospect, 'Living with the Enemy' was possibly not the most chivalrous piece of prose I have ever written. However, names were changed to protect the innocent and I tried to keep the gruesome detail to a minimum (I had the restraint not to mention the dressing gown pocket incident). I showed Dee the piece for her approval before sending it off, and, while not entirely comfortable with having her favourite pet's personality deconstructed in a national pub-lication, she had to admit that my argument added up. It was she, after all, who had told me that The Actor and The Bear had 'unnervingly similar' personalities, and she found it difficult not to admit that, if you were a human who'd been placed in a cat's body with the express purpose of sabotaging a relationship, with all the physical powers and limitations of your new species, you probably would have acted quite a lot like The Bear had during his fortnight in our care.

As for The Bear himself, he appeared during my final couple of proofreading sessions, settling down into my lap and beginning to purr wetly and powerfully, his gaze alternating between my face and the computer screen. This was unsettling, particularly as Dee had told me adamantly that he didn't 'do' laps, but I suppose it was exactly the kind of behaviour you'd expect from a jilted bloke pretending to be a cat.

In truth, I had never met The Actor. From what Dee had told me, he sounded like a decent sort of bloke, if a bit on the intense side. Dee no longer socialised with him, if you discounted conversations regarding pet custody, and by all accounts he was now in a new relationship of his own and had no knowledge of Dee's love life. On the other hand, we had heard suspiciously little from him since his hospitalisation. And was it just me, or did I see The Bear's face darken when I typed the phrase 'failed thespian' before reconsidering and deleting it?

I went to bed that night with more on my mind than in it. Would we ever hear from The Actor again? What did the future hold for me and the small, scheming cat for whom I was starting to feel a strange amount of love? And if The Bear wasn't really The Actor in disguise, and was just an unusually sensitive, perceptive animal with advanced reading skills, would he view my latest act against him as the ultimate betrayal?

It must have been about 3 a.m. by the time I finally drifted off, and it must have been about 3.05 by the time The Bear made the first of his patented, incessant broken smoke alarm noises, and about 3.09 by the time Janet began to headbutt me on the nose: an action in which I delighted, despite the repeated way it interrupted my sleep, and the knowledge that it was really just his way of explaining to me in no uncertain terms that it was time to go out and hit the town and there was nothing I nor any other stinkin' human could, like, do about it, man. Being the only human resident of the flat who didn't tend to sleep as soundly as a character from an Anne Rice novel, I could see that it was perfectly logical that I should be the one to tend to nocturnal feline needs, and, after two weeks, I knew the drill: put The Bear in kitchen. Lock kitchen door. Go back in kitchen to check window is locked and all other escape routes are barred. Open sash window in bedroom. Watch whilst furry bottom exits sash window. Listen whilst furry bottom lands with thump on roof of living room window of stuffy retired colonel downstairs. Shut window. Check window. Open kitchen door. Offer The Bear appeasing snack and try to reason with him about the drawbacks of a nomadic life.

The difference was that today had been the first really hot day of the year. I've always been a poor sleeper in warm weather, and now I wondered what harm it could do to re-open the window. Surely just a couple of inches couldn't hurt?

'Do you mind if I let a bit of air in?' I asked Dee.

'Calculus, I think. Or probably Thomson and Thompson.'

Dee often talked about characters from the *Tintin* comic books in her sleep; it was one of the innumerable things I loved about her.

'I said, "Do you mind if I let some air in"?'

'He is in, isn't he? You're talking about Snowy, aren't you?'

Taking this as a 'yes', I moved towards the window, thinking, 'Just an inch and a half – that would be okay, wouldn't it?'

He couldn't have timed his move more perfectly. I'd
sunk, finally, deliciously, to the bottom of sleep's well, so I
didn't see the escape itself, but I heard it. It even woke Dee
up. It was the sound of a rare kind of urgency: the noise of
a small soldier charging over the top, the noise of a rat up
a drainpipe, a Bear down a drainpipe . . . the noise of all or
nothing. By the time I'd registered it, my body was at the
window, even if my head was still on the pillow. But by
then all that was left was the hum of traffic, the distant
scuttle of paws, and the tiny, yawning gap into the night
air.

I often wonder where The Bear went for the five and a
half weeks that followed. Four days after his escape, The
Actor called to say he was ready to collect him, and Dee
gave him the bad news. Thankfully, she had the tact not
to add 'It was all my new boyfriend's fault' and 'By the
way, I should also point out that he thinks The Bear isn't
a cat at all, but actually you in disguise . . .' If The Bear
did make it back to The Actor's place, The Actor wasn't
telling.

It's possible, of course, that The Bear just got stuck in a
shed or garage, or a troubled pensioner smelling of catnip
temporarily kidnapped him, but, when I think of that
period, I like to think of a collection of littlest hobo-type
images, perhaps soundtracked by The Byrds' 'Wasn't Born
to Follow': The Bear setting off into the early dawn; stopping at the all-night garage for a packet of Benson and
Hedges; getting the tube to Central London; posing for
snapshots pretending to bite the heads off pigeons in
Trafalgar Square, busking outside St Paul's; moving into a
flat-share with some crusties in Camden; falling in with

the wrong crowd; getting embroiled in a bungled heist in an aviary; then, finally, being forced to sell his body among the strays of Canning Town in order to raise the funds to get the Docklands Light Railway back to Blackheath.

There was, however, no time for such romanticism back then. I was distraught. For more than an hour every morning and evening, I would walk the neighbourhood, feeling false elation at every flash of distant tail or black bin liner. Suddenly, the embarrassment of shouting 'Bear, Bear!' at the top of my voice in front of a gang of Lewisham teenagers in hoodies seemed unimportant.

My apologies to Dee were profuse but, of the two of us, she was able to deal with The Bear's disappearance more philosophically. She'd realised by now that he was a cat who beat back his own path and there was little she could do about it. I'd begun to realise this too, but I missed our capricious relationship. Certainly, I loved Janet. You could level few complaints at a cat that would crumple into an obedient heap at your feet with the mere Vulcan-ish touch of a finger to a spot on the left side of his neck, but sometimes I couldn't help yearning for a challenge. Why had I not taken more time to appreciate those hard-won sessions with the clingy alter ego known as 'Koala Bear', or the way one of his ears would crinkle slowly down at my touch when he was in one of his better moods?

The Bear going AWOL presented a much bigger problem for our future – one that neither of us wanted to think about, but that we could not put off indefinitely. That spring, we had been on our first holiday together, to Norfolk: a place I'd always loved and where Dee had spent the first decade of her life, which, we could not help but notice, even in the booming market of 2001, had some very reasonable property prices. We'd both fallen head over heels for it once again, and formulated a crazy plan: in the autumn, Dee would quit her job and we would get married; then, very shortly afterwards, we would head up the M11 to set up home in a rural part of Britain where we knew not one living soul.

Dee and I have always been impulsive, and this has often been our downfall, but there was plenty of logic behind our decision. Not long before meeting me, Dee had been hit over the head with wirecutters and had her wallet snatched by two prostitutes whilst walking down a street in east London at 8 a.m. The encounter had left her with permanent head injuries, and, ever since, she had not felt completely comfortable walking around the capital. Every morning when she set off for work, I worried about her terribly. One day, an idiot stockbroker pushing his way onto a too-full tube swung his hard briefcase onto the side of her head. The same afternoon I received a phone call from one of the editors at the magazine where Dee worked, wondering why she hadn't returned after lunch. Half an hour later, she arrived at our front door, a dreamy, concussed expression on her face, not remembering that, when she had decided to take the afternoon off, she had neglected to tell any of her fellow employees.

Both of us had fond memories of growing up in rural areas, yet simultaneously felt that we'd not quite appreciated country life as much as we should have. For my part, my recent decision to take a metaphorical foot out of the sometimes fetid waters of the music industry somehow was not enough – I wanted to get away physically as well. Having recently been commissioned to write my first book, I liked the idea of tapping away at my keyboard in a place where I could be alone with my thoughts with only the sound of a distant sheep and the burble of a nearby stream in the background. If not that, then at least somewhere without too many Starbucks coffeehouses or second-hand bookshops to distract me. The move was still several weeks away, but if by then The Bear hadn't returned, we both knew we wouldn't be able to leave without him. We were haunted by visions of him returning to an empty flat: the saddest, wettest nose and eyes in south London pressed to the window.

That the idea of kittens would eventually be postulated by one of us, as an extra part of our country plan, was inevitable. Put two well-suited cat lovers, neither of whom has any immediate wish to procreate, in a whirlwhind romantic situation, and give them the promise of a garden of their own, and how could it not? That the suggestion first came up during The Bear's long vacation, however, probably had a lot to do with my continuing need to atone for my mistake with the window. It was that feeling of Wanting to Save All the Cats again – that same one I'd been experiencing ever since that day almost three years before when the Monty Whistle Bird mocked me outside my parents' house. If my suspicious, meddling behaviour and neglect had added to Britain's overflowing population of strays, a bit of compensatory adoption was the least I could do.

When our cat-mad friends, Steve and Sue, came home with a winningly insouciant tabby called Molly and told us that her mum was about to give birth to a second litter of kittens any day, a few more tails around the house became an intrinsic part of any discussion about our new home. We told ourselves in no uncertain terms that these would and could not be 'new' Bears. Neither were they going to usurp Janet in any way. That said, Dee was excited, and I was too – and not, I assured her, for the reason that I was planning to use water to spike our new little friends' hair into mohicans in the way that Steve did with Molly when he was bored.

'Kittens,' Dee would turn to me and say, out of nowhere, as the day came closer.

'Kittens,' I would reply.

We were worrying about The Bear, and I was not quite back in Dee's good books, but we were also beginning to relax and look forward to our new life. That relaxation, however, was our big mistake.

I should have realised that The Bear had an instinctive, telepathic understanding of our schedule, and that geography would prove to be no obstacle to this. Another four weeks on his Orwellian tramp trail, and he would have been returning to an unpleasant twelve-legged surprise. Another eight, and we would have been gone, meaning that, if he were looking for warmth, processed meat and succour, he would have been having to make nice with a raucous Greek family and their vociferous beagle. That the day of his return was also the day of the belated publication of my article, 'Living with the Enemy', was uncanny. I'd just returned from the newsagent when I saw the small, paranoid creature scuttling across our communal garden. At first, I mistook it for some kind of ferret or weasel. I am pretty sure that both would have given off a more appealing odour than the one The Bear did when, a few seconds later, I arrived at the front door to let him in.

For the next three hours, he barely let me out of sight nor sticky grasp – proof of a long-held theory of mine that the amount of love a cat is able to offer at any given time always stands in direct proportion to how dirty it is. His entire body communicated his relief, all the way to that ever-expressive tail of his (see below): an instrument that so often before had seemed like the punctuation mark to his doomy internal monologue. Every few minutes, I would feel overcome by relief and affection and bend down to give him a kiss, then, getting a whiff pitched somewhere between death and cabbage, think better of it.

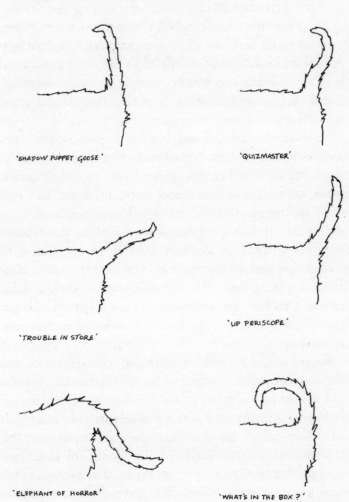

'SHADOW PUPPET GOOSE'

'QUIZMASTER'

'TROUBLE IN STORE'

'UP PERISCOPE'

'ELEPHANT OF HORROR'

'WHAT'S IN THE BOX?'

After so long being the bad guy, it was an additional relief to be able to call Dee and give her the good news. I had not braved a journey to one of London's seedier alcoves and rescued The Bear from the clutches of an evil underworld employer. I had not dived in front of a moving car to save his life. I had not even climbed a ladder and coaxed him down from the high branches of a tree. But when he had scuttled across that lawn, desperate for a bowl of food and a clean, warm human on which to subtly deposit the strange viscous green substance stuck to his left flank, I had been there. And that meant something.

Dee was, of course, elated, but her happiness was tempered with ambivalence. Now The Bear was back, it simply meant that he would be gone again all the sooner. Was this how it was going to be for ever: The Bear shunted between homes like an unwanted child? Would she ever be able to fully lavish the love she wanted to on him, in the knowledge that he was truly her cat? Another tense phone call between her and The Actor followed, and it was decided that it would be kindest for all concerned to do the deed quickly. Dee had just one hour to lavish her grudgingly received affection onto The Bear before he was packed into his luggage.

We had long since realised that the merest sight of a conventional cat basket would send him fleeing for the nearest nook or cranny, so our tactic was to use the pyramid-topped biodegradable equivalent that our Norwegian vet had given to Dee and in which The Bear had been transported to us, two months previously. I volunteered for the task, knowing that he would view it as yet another betrayal. The ensuing struggle proved that, while you might not be able to

put The Bear in a cultural or social box, you could definitely put him in a cardboard one, given dexterous enough
hands and a skilfully placed bowl of evaporated milk.

Some people think the look of a dog that's been wronged
is one of life's most crushing sights. These people have never
known true heartbreak and are clearly labouring under the
misapprehension that the spectrum of animal emotion can
be summarised by drawing a frown, then turning it upside
down. Throw Spot or Chutney a ball or a squeaky rubber
chicken, and move on – you'll be back in the big panting
simpleton's good books in no time. But when you've
wronged a cat, you know you're going to be hearing about it
for some time. It's doubtful that last look The Bear gave me
as I closed the cardboard flaps will ever quite leave my
memory bank. I can still see the eyes now: simultaneously
wide and beseeching, yet slitted and scheming. That inim-
itable ear curled down again, but its fold seemed to signify
something different: a resolute internal tightening. Cats'
mouths don't communicate much, but if there was a way of
shaping your muzzle to convey the sentiment 'One day
when you're asleep, I'm going to creep into your room and
cut you', this was it.

But I was not viewing The Bear as my adversary now. Far
from it. The last time I'd opened that box I'd been a Cat
Man. I had my cat history, cat issues, even. But now, something had tipped. I had surrendered. I had no idea whether
The Bear and I would meet again, but I hoped we did. And
if we did, I knew we would do so on his terms. I could call it
my gaff, because I had taken out my first mortgage, but we
would both know I was kidding myself. We could say that I
provided the food, so I made the rules, but that would just
be merely a front we would put on to curry acceptance in
the wider world. I was going to be his.

SOME RANDOM SELECTIONS FROM
THE CAT DICTIONARY: PART I

Argle

The noise that accompanies the eradication – or attempted eradication – of an ear mite.

Catiquette

The ancient and mysterious social law that governs the cat universe and allows multiple cold-blooded killing machines to live in relative harmony, frequently under the same roof. When is it considered good form to steal an older moggy's favourite spot on a favourite chair? What exactly makes it okay to virtually insert your nose into a fellow cat's rear end one day, and a passing sniff an outright offence less than twenty-four hours' later? In a hungry gaggle of six of Norfolk's most duplicitous, randomly thrown-together pusses, who decides who gets priority at the dinner table, and how? If you've sprayed a microscopic bit of piss on a curtain, why does that make you 'well hard' in the environs of that room, but only 'a bit of a big girl' as soon as you step over the carpet divider? How does a cat implicitly understand what a 'garden' is, and where it begins and ends? Humans remain in the dark about all this, but catiquette provides the answers.

ES Pee

The telepathic process that leads a cat to only get properly settled on its owner's stomach in the moments when that owner is most desperate for the toilet.

Furmat's Last Theorem

The inarguable mathematical law that states that a cat's affection will rise and fall in direct proportion to the dirt on its body at the time.

Nuggin

The act of pushing one's cold wet nose into one's owner's hand or knuckle. Largely thought of as a gesture of affection, but sometimes given a bad press, owing to its alternative nickname, 'Losing the Snot'.

Nuggbutt

Essentially a larger version of the nuggin, involving the full upper-head area. Usually employed at times when jellied meat is in the immediate vicinity.

Reflectytime

Those meditative I-should-really-have-a-newspaper-here moments on the litter tray or the freshly hoed soil when one's hard-set veneer of dignity is momentarily dropped, a certain faraway dreaminess comes over the eyes and, just for twenty or thirty seconds, all in the world is right.

Uwookwack

The wobbly lipped noise made by a cat when it looks out of a window and sees a wood pigeon 'acting up'.

Out of the Bag

'So what do you think? Should we do it?'
  'It's a tough one, but I know what you mean.'
  'They'll be all right, won't they?'
  'Yeah. I think.'
  'What do you mean "I *think*"?'
  'I just mean yeah, they'll be fine.'
  'You don't, though, do you?'
  'It's just . . . '
  'It's not too early to leave, is it?'
  'No.'
  'And we've had a great time.'
  'Oh yeah, totally. And it's almost like being on holiday where we live anyway.'
  'Yeah.'
  'Yeah.'
  'Yeah.'
  'So . . . I guess we ought to start getting packed, then?'
  'Make sure you save some of that leftover parma ham for Shipley when you're emptying the fridge.'

There is no great mystery to the origins of the term 'honey-moon'. The 'honey' bit refers to the sweetness of the first weeks of marriage, the 'moon' bit refers to the length of this period and its inevitable waning. A few of the finer details about honeymoons have changed since the sixteenth century, when the term was coined – a period when package deals to the Maldives were notably thin on the ground – but the time frame has remained fairly constant. In other words, you do the honeying bit as early within the moon as possi-ble: a splendid idea, not least because it allows you to have a bit of irresponsible fun before your first argument in the paint department of B&Q.

Dee and I decided to take a more contrary approach. When we got married, at Marylebone Register Office, in the autumn of 2001, four days before moving to Norfolk, we agreed to delay the accompanying holiday for four and half months. The other unusual thing about our honey-moon was that it lasted three days fewer than it was supposed to.

The first part of this behaviour is fairly easily explained. By this point, Brewer, Prudence and Shipley, our new cats, were still barely bigger than my hands, and very nearly as clumsy. When you're arriving in an alien part of the coun-try with three 12-week-old kittens and their possibly retarded step-sibling, the last thing you want to do is leave those kittens in a cattery or alone in your new house while you jet off to the other side of the world.[3] Not only that, the stress of organising a wedding, a last minute, knotty bit of

---

[3] Okay, so maybe 'other side of the world' is a slight exaggeration, but Devon's a long drive from Norfolk.

conveyancing and moving furniture from our flat, Dee's parents' house in Brighton and my parents' house in Nottingham had left its physical marks on both of us.

To the irritable bowel syndrome from which I'd suffered all my adult life, I could recently add a sore throat and a particularly virulent pair of recurring ear infections. The latter had proved to be beyond three different doctors and three increasingly strong sets of antibiotics, and I'm sure weren't just a natural byproduct of having spent too long reviewing Simply Red albums for a living. I'd been hoping that the clean country air would quickly clear them up, but somewhere on my third sleep-deprived trip up the A11 I couldn't help noticing that I'd gone deaf in both ears and that a dark purple substance had started oozing out of my head. I would have been more concerned, but I was a bit too busy worrying about the giant mutant strain of Norfolk deer that I kept hallucinating in front of the windscreen and a resurgence of some even more mutant whooping cough that I thought I'd got rid of around the time of my eleventh birthday. The woeful sack of a man that flopped down among an ocean of boxes that night was hardly what you'd call a 'husband', never mind the kind that you'd want to whisk off in a hurry for early-marital jollies.

When we did finally make it to our honeymoon near Dartmoor the following February, we were in far better spirits (the purple stuff was long gone by then). Our holiday cottage was cosy, the pool and sauna were effectively all ours, and we had a good laugh at the comments in the guest book ('pool too cold for baby Caspar'), but from the moment three days in when I wondered aloud if the cats were okay, nothing was ever quite as relaxed. It's funny in these situations how quickly 'What if Bob Potter next door has lost his key to our backdoor?' can escalate into 'What if

the cat-flap gets locked by mistake?' and 'What if Janet
jumps up on the hob and accidentally turns the gas on with
his tail?' Undoubtedly, Dee and I were egging one another
on. Equally undoubtedly, I was the one who started it. I
nearly always am.

If they're to succeed, all co-owners of cats must go
through a period where they learn to mould themselves
around one another's habits. It had taken a while for our
roles to become properly entrenched, but the signs had been
there right back during those first few nights together, when
Janet had begun his rigorous regime of training me to get up
at 5 a.m. to feed him. By the time we'd become owners of
Brewer, Shipley and Prudence as well, the routine was firmly
in place: less 'good cop, bad cop' and more 'wet pushover
cop, slightly more assertive cop'.

When we arrived at the eighties housing estate in
Romford the previous September and met Mick and John,
the two gay *Big Brother* fans whose tabby had just had a
second litter, any impartial outsider would soon have
worked out who was wearing the hair-flecked trousers in
our relationship. As Dee and our friends Steve and Sue
talked to Mick and John about the strength of the gay vote
in *Big Brother* and their joy at the victory of BB2's Brian
Dowling, I strolled out into the garden and zoned in on the
tiny, somewhat Yoda-like kitten leaping manically over the
ornamental pond. We'd arrived with the intention of
coming away with two new cats, at the most, and we'd
already decided on Brian Two (black and white, fluffyish)
and Brian Four (tabby, more fluffyish), but it was me who
pushed for the 'bonus ball' inclusion of the sleek-furred,
irrepressible Brian Seven (or, in Steve's words, 'the ugly
black runty one').

A few weeks later, though, when Brian Two (now

Prudence) began to soil the duvet and Brian Four (now Brewer) and Brian Seven (now Shipley) began a bout of skilfully timed tag team claw-sharpening, I realised it was time to get tough.

'Now,' I explained to Shipley. 'That's really not on. That's a very old chair you're tearing up there. It used to belong to Dee's grandma.'

'It's much more effective if you just growl at them,' said Dee.

Dee and I had always laughed at the middle-class soft touch dads: the floppy men we used to see in shops in Blackheath Village, patiently asking little Sebastian or Ciabatta how they thought it made the octogenarian next to them *feel* when they stood on her bunions and didn't say sorry. Was it my destiny to become one of these people? I hoped not. It would have been absurd to deny that my talents as a disciplinarian of small cats probably did provide a fairly good guide to my potential as a disciplinarian of small humans, but I was sure there was no affection being displaced or misplaced here.

It riled me when acquaintances and family would suggest that my cats represented some kind of trial run for parenthood. What rankled most about this was the way it carried with it the implicit suggestion that, were Dee and I to procreate, we would happily change our tune and leave our moggies out with the following week's recycling. I love elephants and donkeys too, and, in the unlikely event I had enough room to own one, I would feed it regularly, give it a nickname, and stroke and pat it, and indulge its every whim. Would that make that a child substitute too? No: it would make it a very big, lovable, overindulged animal, in much the same way my cats were smaller, lovable, overindulged animals. That said, I can understand the slight look of horror in the eyes of my mum – a person who'd obviously made up her mind that the primary reason her only son and his wife would have moved out of the big city was to immediately settle down and start a family – the day she arrived at our new cottage to find me waiting for her at the door with Shipley in my arms, fast asleep in an upside down 'cradle' position.

I did manage to keep my soppiness hidden some of the time – sometimes without having to try too hard. If Surreal Ed had had any doubts that I was making a gradual exit from our 4 a.m. danceathons, I'm sure they were quashed during the sleepless night he spent on my sofa bed getting his ever-restless feet chased by Brewer, Shipley and Prudence, but I still got the sense there was a part of my home life about which Ed, never much of a cat fan, remained in denial. Call me presumptuous, but on certain occasions he just seemed to be missing something: one of these being the time, not long before we left London, when he sat in my living room and told me, in hopeful, sympathy stimulating tones, about the latest girl he'd dumped. 'What went wrong?' I asked him, as Shipley perched happily on my shoulder and began to lick my ear. 'Oh,' he replied. 'She was too obsessed with her bloomin' cats. What can blokes like us do, eh, Tom?'

Even more oblivious to the situation were Dee's parents. Every time they visited us, they would look at me with increasing sympathy, as if to acknowledge the strain it must have been for me to put up with their daughter's ever-growing self-indulgent collection of filthy carpet shredders. Happy to be cast in the role of the evolved, understanding husband, I would raise my eyes and smile in a way that I hoped offered no firm opinion on the matter, but suggested an overall patience and gave no hint that I had just recently inaugurated our very own household Cat of the Month award.[4] It was the kind of subterfuge you learned a lot of when you lived in close proximity to whiskers.

Dee's mum, Oriel, is one of the most philanthropic people you could hope to meet: unfailingly conscientious about the environment, a nurturer of disadvantaged birdlife, constantly involved in a dozen different forms of charity work. Her compassion, however, tends to peter out rather dramatically when the subject is four-legged and kills sparrows for sport. When Dee had first sheepishly admitted to her that we'd got some new kittens and made the mistake of mentioning they were proving a bit of handful, Oriel was quick to put forward the helpful suggestion that we 'drown them in a bucket'. Dee had been so worried about her mum's reaction to our new hairy lodgers that she'd actually fudged the figures slightly.

'So how many cats is that now?' Oriel had asked.

'Oh, just the three,' replied Dee.

When I questioned Dee on her deception and expressed concern about the potential repercussions, she explained that, during future visits from her mum and dad, our three all-black cats could be passed off as one. I remained sceptical, but, sure enough, over the course of three days in Oriel and Chris's company, no questions were asked. The only extra precaution we'd needed to take was to make sure a maximum of three of our five moggies were in one room at any given time. After a while, we didn't even bother doing that. If you overlooked the time that Shipley clambered all over Chris's first run edition of James Thurber's, *The Thurber*

---

[4] Having at one point put forward the suggestion of mounting the winner's photo on the fridge in a magnetic frame and photoshopping a baseball cap on their head, I reconsidered and decided this would be going too far.

Carnival and tried to put his bottom in his face, felines quite simply didn't feature on my parents-in-laws' radar.

Did I say five cats? I did. Did I mean to say four? I did not. Did I say three *black* cats? I did. The Bear's surprise arrival back in our lives came at a typically choice moment. At the moment The Actor called, Dee and I had been very carefully trying to carry a duvet from our bedroom to the bathroom without allowing the pool of Prudence's urine in the centre of it to tip onto the floor. We'd been living in the village of Brunton for five days by then and each of those days had revealed another dozen or so defects in our perfect cottage. We'd got on very well with the people who sold it to us, taken them for rational human beings and fussed over their cats, so when, we wondered, exactly *had* they had the bad acid trip that led to them deciding it would be a good idea to paint the light switches into a permanent 'off' position using bright yellow paint? Had the stainless steel kitchen sink been painted in dark blue gloss in some kind of schizophrenic panic the last few weeks of their residence, or were we just too dazzled by our fantasies of country life to notice it?

While Dee had gone to work on the gaping hole in the bedroom floor, I'd started on the garden, where the compost heap soon turned out to be nothing more than a front for a minor nuclear waste dump containing old golf bags, half-filled cans of oil and nameless bottles of bright purple fluid with big pictures of skulls with crosses through them, broken glass and what we realised, in retrospect, was almost certainly the asbestos roof of an ancient aircraft hangar. It was almost a relief when Prudence decided that, much as she could see the litter tray made a lot of practical sense, she felt, on the whole, the enveloping embrace of goose down provided a much more relaxed environment in which to empty her bladder. At least it gave us a distraction from the fungus growing in the haemorrhoid-pink shagpile carpet in the upstairs bathroom.

'Er. We have a slight hitch,' said Dee, returning from the phone. 'How do you fancy going to London to pick up a package?'

The way he'd told it to Dee, The Actor had not had much choice in the matter: his work opportunity in Australia was a last minute one, and involved an immediate flight. Nonetheless, demanding that his ex-girlfriend, a non-driver, travel 120 miles to collect The Bear the very same afternoon seemed a mite inconsiderate. Did he know when he'd be back? He didn't. *Would* he be coming back at all? Er, he wasn't sure, actually.

'Anyway, that's it,' Dee explained to me. 'No more toing and froing. This is the last time. He's our cat now.'

Considering my dual ear infection and cough, it is obvious that the decision to zoom down to London at 8 p.m. that same night was made by a man who'd been rendered senseless by spending too long in the Relocation Zone. If I was being truthful, I'd first noticed the slight unbalanced feeling in our Ford Fiesta the previous night, but I'd quickly dismissed it from my mind. It was just another thing on a long list of jobs, something to think about after I'd found the kettle and been to the hardware store to get the stuff to block up the hole in the porch where the water was coming in and been to IKEA to buy six replacement reserve duvets for Prudence to soil. I'd barely reached the Norfolk–Suffolk border by the time everything started wobbling and I heard the 'ftt-ftt' sound coming from the front left of the car.

My dad did once show me how to change a tyre. I was thirteen at the time, and probably busy checking out my bad eighties quiff in the wing mirror, but I'm sure I was half-

listening. If I really tried, I could probably have dredged some
of the information back up from the cobwebbed recesses of
my brain, but in view of the fact I didn't much fancy getting
my upper body jammed under a Ford Fiesta in a dark
Norfolk layby, I did the same thing a lot of other bookish,
cat-loving men of Generation X would have done: I phoned
the RAC. While I waited for them to arrive, I called Dee,
and the two of us put her original plan back in place: the
one that involved calling our friend Michael and asking if
The Actor could drop The Bear with him for a couple of
days, until we would be in a fit state to make it back to
Blackheath.

I couldn't say I'd been looking forward to meeting The
Actor, but neither could I pretend that the encounter didn't
have its supernatural appeal: a bit like meeting Batman and
Bruce Wayne in the same room at the same time. Once
again, it was hard not to feel there was a higher Bear power
at work here: The Bear did not want this, so it had not happened.

But if my pointy-eared nemesis was in a mystical frame of
mind, he might well meet his match later that night. A folk
musician with a penchant for magic herbalism and lyrics
about burning scarecrows, Michael's many very spiritual,
very 1971 beliefs included the one that animals could not be
'owned'. In spite of this, he enjoyed sharing the big dribbling
love of a gigantic, wandering ginger cat called Ramases with
an old man in the flat above him.

For safety's sake, Michael had made sure that Ramases
wasn't around when The Actor dropped The Bear off, but
he'd neglected to check behind the horse's head mask – a
favourite prop of Michael's, often worn on stage during his

songs 'Power to the Pixies' and 'Reality is a Fantasy' – on the shelf above his bed. As soon as The Bear had crept fearfully from his travelling polymer prison onto the bedspread, the more established cat had wasted no time in pouncing, landing on the bed with a 'Browwwaaagh' noise. His vision engulfed by flaming fur and bright green eyes, The Bear had scuttled away, eventually making himself comfortable at the back of the wardrobe, amidst Michael's collection of medieval capes.

'He's been there ever since,' Michael told us two days later, when Dee and I arrived to collect him. 'Actually, no, that's not true. He did come out once, when I was boiling some broccoli.'

'Ooh yes,' said Dee. 'That's one of his vices.'

'I thought you said the only thing he ate apart from cat food and cold meats was curry,' I said.

'Well, yeah, that is sort of true. But there was this one day when he freaked out and ate some broccoli and then a Pop Tart. Or maybe it was the Pop Tart first. I can't remember.'

'Well, he was very affectionate,' said Michael. 'I don't think I've ever felt anything like it from a cat. It scared me a bit. I actually had to have a sit down afterwards. Oh yeah, another weird thing, as well. I thought the battery had run out on my smoke alarm because it kept making this weird noise. It was ages before I remembered I didn't even have a smoke alarm and realised it was The Bear.'

Thanking Michael for his good deed, we made our way back to the car. Dee had coaxed The Bear into the cat box on her own this time. I couldn't see him through the gaps, but I sensed he knew I was there. To help the journey pass, Michael had loaned us a tape of *The Garden of Jane Delawney*, a folk album made in 1970 by a group called Trees. The first line on the album is, 'Country air, wrap yourself around me.'

You wouldn't exactly have called it driving music, but it was perfect for travelling to a folklore-rich place like Norfolk on a misty autumn night: all ghostly whispers, elfin melodies and creeping vine guitars. It was easy for a fanciful, overoptimistic person to get carried away about his new rural life and start thinking about the country horror novel he would write, to which this would provide the sound-track.

For a while, the unrelenting 'meeyeeooop' noise from the back seat added an extra layer of spookiness to the melodies, but by about track five it started to sound a bit psychotic, so we turned it off and decided to listen to *The Archers* instead.

That had been almost six months before, and in the inter-vening period, Dee and I had taken one reality check after another about country life. We had done nothing as tedious as 'research' before moving to Brunton: our original feeling had simply been that it was in Norfolk, and Norfolk was all lovely, wasn't it? Well, yes, to an extent, but moving to a vil-lage ten miles from the nearest supermarket, the bulk of whose employment was provided by a nearby remand centre, with only one driving licence between the two of you, was always going to be a culture shock after living in a city where all your materialistic desires were on tap, day and night. Clinging to our idea of a rural idyll, we often couldn't even find a rural Lidl. And why had nobody thought to tell us that in the Norfolk countryside winters last eight times as long as they do in London? I'm sure I'd been reading too many of those 'Life in the Day' columns in the back of the *Sunday Times Magazine* where successful rustic creative types talked about getting up with the dawn chorus, working for five hours, then spending the afternoon going on country walks and pottering about their herb garden, but back in Blackheath I'd begun to kid myself I would be moving not just to a whole new place, but a whole new time zone, where days lasted three times as long.

These *real* days dragged on in an entirely different way. There were still deadlines to meet and email to keep up with and a mortgage to pay, just as there had been in Blackheath, but there was also DIY to do, and mud – most of it brought in on twenty small but surprisingly absorbent paws – and no pub or club containing half a dozen friends where you could forget about it all, and driving, endless driving, and tiny Victorian cottage windows with the dark, dark, interminable night beyond them. In five months, I don't think I'd pottered once.

The autumn of 2001 was a seductive time for a London resident to be nurturing a small-scale Back to the Land fantasy. Moving to the country and getting it wrong has become a cliché now, but back then early evening television was newly inundated with programmes seemingly telling city dwellers that all they needed to do was look fifty miles or more beyond the M25 and buy a giant farmhouse and they would never need to work, get in a traffic jam or have their vision sullied by a branch of Sock Shop ever again.

These shows were not the catalyst for our move, but they acted as a form of affirmation – and the fact that the houses in them always seemed to feature a contented sleeping cat on the bed helped, too. When we'd stood on the pavement outside the bar where we'd had our wedding party that October night, friend after friend had told us that, what with the attack on New York a few weeks ago, they didn't feel safe in London any more, and they'd probably be hot on our tails in a few months' time. We knew this was largely the drink and the occasion talking, but that did not mean we

didn't like the sound of it. We felt less like we were embark-
ing on a new life and more like we were the team leaders
of an unusually domesticated outward bound expedition,
scouting out the territory before the rest of our group made
their way through the brush to join us. If friends did not ask
us to reserve them a seat in the local pub, they talked to
us as if we were pioneers, setting off for nineteenth-century
Montana to set up camp amongst ignoble tribes and cowboys.

'You're so *brave*,' I remember a couple of people saying.

Were we? Really? That probably depends just how wussy
and middle class your criterion is for bravery. It wasn't as
if we were off to trade in all our earthly possessions and follow
the Bhagwan Rajneesh with a new loosely clad surrogate
family. We weren't starting our own smallholding and making
our own yoghurt, or renovating a dilapidated monastery.
We'd even chickened out of our original plan to buy a goat
for the back garden. We were about to move to a small,
slightly neglected detached house in a cut-price area of
Norfolk to raise some cats, with a view to writing a few books
(me), selling some old things on the Internet (Dee), and, if
we got a chance, enjoying a bit of golf and horse riding in our
spare time.

Both of us had done this before, anyway, hadn't we? We'd
lived in the countryside for the majority of our childhoods.
But living in the countryside under the shelter of your parents' roof is very different to living in the countryside in
your first house in your mid-twenties with no friends or relatives within a sixty-mile radius. I may have lived in
London for less than three years in total, but the place had
been shaping my social habits for a lot longer than that, and
Norfolk's particular pace of life required some acclimatisa-
tion. When you're used to getting most of your mail franked
a couple of hundred yards from Oxford Circus tube station,

walking into your village post office and listening to the following ten-minute conversation – and I *mean* ten minutes – playing out is always going to throw you off balance:

Man 1: 'Keeping well, John?'

Man 2: 'Keeping well, Mick.'

Man 1: 'Keeping well. That's the way you doos it.'

Man 2: 'Certainly is, bore. Certainly is. How about yourself?'

Man 1: 'Ah, not so bad. Not so bad.'

Lengthy pause.

Man 2 (pulling face of intense concentration suggestive of Mathematical Olympiad): 'Not so bad, eh? That's the way you doos it. Lovely job.'

Man 1: 'Certainly is. Certainly is.'

Man 2: 'Making much money at the moment?'

Man 1: 'Ah, not so bad, not so bad. Just taken on a little job for my sister's bloke.'

Man 2: (squinting into middle distance in manner of someone who has seen a squirrel in a top hat on the other side of the road breaking into his car): 'Hmmm. Well, you gots to sometime, haven't you?'

Man 1: 'You can say that again, my friend.'

Man 2: 'Easy does it.'

Lengthy pause.

Man 1: 'Easy does it. You got that right, my friend.'

Another lengthy pause in which both parties make 'hmm' and 'nnn' noises at one another.

Man 2: 'All right, Mick. Best be getting on. Take it easy, bore.'

Man 1: 'Will do. You yourself too, my friend. Steady as you go now, bore.'

Man 2: 'Ooh yes. Steady as I go. You know me. That's the way you doos it.'

Man 1: 'Ha. You can say that again, John.'

When Dee and I did eventually get served that day, the postmaster looked at Dee's six variously shaped, flawlessly packed inland eBay packages like she'd just handed him half a dozen unpackaged, unaddressed slices of pizza and asked him to personally hand-deliver them to the Bronx.

'You up at the Murrays' old place?' he said, as he began to violently shake a package containing a 1930s chandelier that Dee had sold to someone in Loughborough.

'That's us!' we said, our grins freezing to our faces.

'The ones with the cats, aren't you?' he asked.

We answered, once again, in the affirmative.

'Stayed on the market a long time, that did.'

It was important not to be scared, we told ourselves. I'd grown up in a couple of ostensibly sinister villages in north Nottinghamshire, after all, and I had never had my body encased in a giant pagan structure or chopped up and served in a hot dog at a local fundraising event, had I? We were not characters in *Straw Dogs* or *The Wicker Man*. Just because the taciturn, vaguely intimidating manner of the postmaster had now been rendered the stuff of cliché by 100 horror films and comedy sketches, that didn't mean he was going to care enough to stop being taciturn and intimidating. This was real English life – the dominant kind. Sleepy. Local. And, okay, just a little bit unsettling. And if it was a little disturbing that he'd heard about us on the village grapevine so quickly, we were learning that 'The Ones with the Cats' wasn't always such a bad label to carry around with you.

We'd first met our next-door neighbour, Bob Potter, when he'd been over to welcome us to the village two or three weeks after we'd moved in. A man in his late sixties with an aura that was simultaneously businesslike and slightly woollen, he wore his former profession – that of secondary school headmaster – across his brow. Any sem-blance of gruffness, however, soon evaporated when a perky Shipley greeted him on his way into our kitchen.

'Ah, cats,' he said, instinctively seeing that Shipley was angling for a gentle pat on the bottom of his spine. 'Love 'em, I do. Proper pets. You get back what you put in. If you go away and want them feeding, just give me or Rosemary a shout.'

It's always nice to have a feline ambassador when you have guests over. That role had traditionally fallen – and still did fall, to an extent, to Janet – but from the moment Shipley had first skipped confidently out into the flat in Blackheath and sniffed the bigger black cat's bottom, he'd made mimicking his step-brother his full-time occupation. There was something very Scrappy-Doo about this. Shipper was already beginning to lose that Yoda look he'd had at eight weeks old, and his newfound gregariousness had already stretched to encompass everyone from Dee's step-grandma to the heavily tanned man – at least, I hoped it was tan – who'd cleared out our sceptic tank.

'You're very friendly, aren't you?' said Bob, upping the pressure of his pats, to Shipley's delight. 'I haven't met this one before, but I think I've met a couple of your others. Another bigger short-haired black one and a little tabby. They both come and stare in through our kitchen window. The black one clears off very quickly, but the tabby one just keeps staring at our Buttercup. She's the youngest of our three. He sometimes presses his nose up so close to the window that he leaves a smear.'

As we got to know Bob better and he continued to report back on the secret lives of our cats, it did not surprise me that The Bear and Prudence were usually the main focus. The Bear had been in a particularly wilful mood since his arrival in Brunton, and, having found a hole in the back of a cupboard in the living room, he'd spent much of the time keeping himself to himself – with the exception of the odd scratching or 'argle' noise – in the esoteric airspace between the living room ceiling and the floorboards of the spare bedroom. But I knew he was not one to take a narrow view of his surroundings and that he would have been careful to take the time to scope out the neighbourhood.

As for Prudence, we'd been wondering why she had a lovelorn air about her, and her nasal functions had been a touch on the leaky, snuffly side since our first week in Brunton, when she'd fallen out of a tree in the garden and cut her nose. Obviously making your first contact with your neighbours through the medium of cat snot was not an ideal scenario, but it was good to know that, in Buttercup, she had a new playmate. It also explained the somewhat forlorn wailing noise that was becoming an increasing part of her night-time ritual. Actually, in view of the fact Buttercup was a boy cat, it probably explained it a little *too* well.

'I've been reading about this,' explained Dee. 'You're supposed to have them spayed when they're five or six months old, but sometimes they can come into heat a bit early. Do you think she's, y'know, calling?'

When we'd chosen the kittens, making sure that one of them was female had been an important part of the process for Dee. If she had indulged me in my campaign for the wild card that was Shipley, it was perhaps partly because she knew that she'd been granted the privilege of first choice. The choosing hadn't taken long, and the deal was sealed when Prudence immediately fell asleep in the crook of her arm. Eschewing gender, my selection criterion had been a little different: I wanted two cats that looked like they would chase a hacky-sack around a room for periods of up to an hour without getting cynical. It's more difficult to tell the gender of a cat from their behaviour when they're very young and I'd already chosen Brewer and Shipley before I was told they were boy cats. That I wanted to name them after a beardy, all-male 1970s stoner folk rock duo was moot: if they had both been girls, I would probably still have named them after a beardy all-male 1970s stoner folk rock duo.

Now, though, it seemed obvious who the blokes around the house were. Brewer's signature throaty exclamation – more of a 'eweow' than a 'meow' – might have been more redolent of a human crèche than the prowling fields of his ancestors, but at five months old, he was already bigger than The Bear and showing a leaning towards wanderlust. Shipley, meanwhile, was getting more sinewy by the day and, if his garrulous meeyapping was not entirely masculine, his deep throat purr gave him the aura of the undersized, geeky kid who can already mysteriously grow sideburns in the fourth year of primary school.

Prudence was not only less muscular and boisterous than her brothers, she was also a bit more high-pitched and high-maintenance (it was a constant source of fascination to me that three cats from the same litter could have such aggressively eclectic voiceboxes). If she was permitted the odd bit of special treatment – an extra bit of wafer thin ham here, an extra soiled duvet there – it was, I was reminded by Dee, only right, since Pruders was the only other woman in a house containing five blokes. I was careful to agree with this at all points and not bring up the subject of women's lib in the cat universe. I could have done without the 2 a.m. wailing sessions in the echoey spare room, though.

'You want to get her done,' said Bob one day, leaning over the fence, as we observed Prudence shinning up a tree in his garden in pursuit of Buttercup.

If I'm completely frank, I have to admit that, had Dee pushed for a Prudence litter, my resolve would have been quick to crumble. Nonetheless, while my feeling on the subject of kittens remained of a fundamentally 'Bring them on!' nature, I could not see any logic to adding to the UK's population of cats, when there were still so many out there that needed rescuing. And much as we'd enjoyed the synchronised wacky races around the living room and the ping pong ball football and the way Prudence and Shipley and Brewer fell asleep afterwards in a perfectly arranged triple-decker pile, the mentally taxing game of Hide the Litter Tray had not been quite so enjoyable, and we were not looking forward to a second heat. Only by moving the box full of granulated clay by increments of an inch every eight hours or so had I finally convinced the three of them that there was nothing inherently primitive about evacuating one's bowels in the open air.

Even now, with the box gone and the 'tray' just a heap of intermingled soil and litter in an unused flower bed at the back of the garden, Brewer didn't seem to quite grasp the age-old tradition of burying your wares: the useless scrape-mime he did over his increasingly virulent packages was a sort of post-excretion cat equivalent of air guitar. Me? I was just glad that none of this was happening indoors any more and taking time to relish the once seemingly unachievable luxury of going to bed without finding tiny bits of clumped grit stuck between my toes. I planned on making it last.

It's always a significant moment in a man's relationship with his cat when he takes it to get its sexual organs nullified. In view of the fact that The Bear could shoot me daggers for the mere crime of getting in his light while he was cleaning his paws, I was thankful that the loss of his testicles was one of the few misdemeanours for which he could not hold me responsible. Brewer and Shipley didn't have his chronic oversensitivity, but the day I picked them up from the local vets – and by 'local' here I mean 'would have taken you half a day's journey on horseback to get to in the nineteenth century' – I could tell from one look in their drugged eyes that there would never be quite the same trust between us again. Their throaty, thankful mewls might have been a way of expressing superficial pleasure that I was there to collect them from the bad place with the knives and the cage, but they disguised something else. That something was the wariness of those who can never go to asleep again entirely certain in the knowledge that something near and dear to them won't be stolen.

But what would really be different for Shipley and Brewer? They'd have one or two less urges, and a slightly lighter feeling around the undercarriage, but that would be about it. Prudence, who followed them two days later, would have the much greater indignity of having to walk around with a fifth of her body shaved, like the result of some malicious game conceived by easily bored children.

Waiting for Dee in the car park as she brought our tabby out after her ordeal, I could tell, even from a distance of thirty yards or more, that my wife looked unusually dejected.

'Poor Prudence,' I said, as Dee slumped down in the passenger seat with a giant sigh. 'Still, she's been brave, hasn't she?'

'Yes, *she* has been brave,' said Dee.

'Perhaps we should give her some of those treats when we get home,' I suggested. 'The ones that look like camel bogeys.'

'Yes, perhaps we should give *her* some of those treats.'

I looked across at Dee. She seemed to be behaving oddly, not like her normal level-headed self. I'd known her to get upset about the hardship endured by her cats in the past – particularly that of The Bear – but this was only a routine operation: a rite of passage, really, kind of like a feline Bar Mitzvah. Her voice seemed fraught, and it scared me slightly.

'Did the vet say anything about her?' I said.

'Oh, he said plenty. But nothing, specifically, about *her*.'

I looked across at her again. She raised her eyebrows at me, and a flash of recognition passed behind my eyes.

'You mean . . .?' I said.

'Yep. I mean . . .'

'But . . .'

'I know.'

'How?'

'I know. But when the vet looked, all the equipment was in evidence. Meat and two veg. What we've got ourselves is a whinging little bloke.'

How could we have allowed this to happen? Was this, when it came right down to it, the kind of people we were? The kind of people who couldn't go on holiday without worrying that one of their cats would switch the hob on with their tail? The kind of people who couldn't change tyres? The kind of people who couldn't accurately distinguish the gender of an everyday household pet? I was now even more certain that I was going to put the goat plan on the back burner.

When we'd been to collect Prudence from her original owners, they'd assured us that she was one of the three of their little Brians who was female. We'd even performed our own check. Admittedly, it had been a bit half-hearted, and had essentially involved nothing more than blowing the hair back in the area in question, but we'd been satisfied with our findings – or lack of them, as it were.

For Dee, the humiliation was twofold, since she'd already been through this once with Janet. 'You would have thought I'd learned that you have to check more thoroughly with hairy cats, wouldn't you?' she said. 'The vet did say that as cat nuts go they were on the small side, but I think he was just trying to make me feel better.'

It was hard to know what to say. For a moment, I considered relating a story about the time an old girlfriend of mine had run to her mum in tears, after mistaking a perfectly natural pinkish growth around her guinea pig's midriff for an inoperable tumour, but I thought better of it. In the end, we spent the remainder of the journey home in stunned silence, but I think, even then, the actions and foibles that had defined the young life of the animal in the basket on Dee's lap were already starting to take on a radically different hue in both of our minds.

The Bear put in a rare appearance when we arrived home. If you ignore the odd cardboard-based disagreement with Shipley – i.e. The Bear wanted to sleep in it, Shipley wanted to chew it – he largely remained aloof and superior around the younger cats, but now, as Prudence crawled his groggy way out of his travel basket, The Bear gave 'her' bottom a good, long sarcastic sniff. If he'd stood up on his hind legs, put on some reading glasses, frowned theatrically and said, 'Now, of course, if you'd come to *me* for advice in the first place . . .' he could not have been more eloquently disapproving.

He'd obviously known the true state of affairs long ago,

but perhaps, like us, he'd also noticed that, equipped with a new gender, Prudence seemed irrevocably altered, as if in the last twenty-four hours he had not only had his biological workings turned upside down but his character with them. As we came to terms with this different persona, we realised it demanded a new name – particularly as it would be far too much hassle to have two boy cats with female monikers to explain to visitors. I quite liked Delawney, but we agreed, without any extraneous toing and froing, on Ralph, after the kid from *The Simpsons*. The inept one who's always wetting himself.

SOME RANDOM SELECTIONS FROM
THE CAT DICTIONARY: PART II

Gribbly bits

The bits of jellified cat meat that escape from the bowl and
weld themselves to hardwood floors and kickboards – sometimes even if you don't have kickboards.

Helping

To offer crucial moral support while one's owner is hard at
work. More popular examples include 'Painting' (brushing
one's tail against some fresh paintwork and leaving a hairy
residue), 'Carrying' (darting in between one's owner's feet
when they are transporting a heavy tray of food between
rooms) and 'Testing for Bacteria' (licking some freshly buttered bread while one's owner's back is turned).

Mousetache

A perfectly placed mouse, held between the teeth in a
strategically horizontal manner (preferably with a slight
downward droop at each end), so as to make the creature's
captor look particularly dashing. Out-of-vogue variations
include 'The Zapata Moustache', 'Sidebirds', and the rare-
but-always-impressive 'Handlebat'.

Muzzlewug

The state of bliss created by the perfect friction of an owner's fingers on a fully extended chin.

Puddings

A particularly furious kind of padding session involving soft human body parts. Also known as 'Marching' or 'Cooking the Dough'.

Purple mist

The special kind of unforgiving cat anger reserved for an owner who has experimented by attaching a lead to its collar.

Quantum physics

The mysterious force allowing a contented cat to fold its limbs, head and torso into an area a quarter of the size of its usual body mass.

Rainy dry paper

Tissues (preferably Sainsbury's Rose-Scented).

Thinking tears

Eye gunk.

Life in the Fast Lane

Every arty family that plunges zealously into country life needs a bloodthirsty neighbour on hand to help them out of a tough spot from time to time. During my final period living in the north-east Midlands with my parents, ours was a man called Frank. Lank of hair and economical of conversation, Frank lived next door and worked as a farmhand a mile or so up the road, but I remember thinking that, despite a certain ageless quality, he seemed a little too old to merit a job description ending in the word 'hand'. Another thing about him that I found slightly unsettling was his habit of popping up from behind hedges on what felt like every occasion I ventured into our garden.

Nonetheless, I had to admit that he came in useful in the aftermath of some of Monty's and The Slink's more heartless maiming exercises. He also proved invaluable in the summer of 1996 when our chickens began to succumb to a variety of unpleasant mishaps.

Personally, I'd never considered chickens as pets. Unlike cats, they didn't purr when you stroked them, and, even in the intellectually challenged field of birdlife, their stupidity was quite astounding. Nonetheless, I soon became attached to the seven bantams that my parents had installed in the coop at the bottom of our garden, particularly Egbert, our comically tiny rooster, whose favourite pastime was sneaking up on my dad in the garden and viciously peck-headbutting the back of his legs. Something I've noticed about chickens, though, is that, when the hard times hit, it's easier to adopt a philosophical stance than it might be with many more resilient pets. When one of them gets snatched by a fox, you get quite cut up about it, but when five die in two weeks, an inbuilt coping mechanism kicks in.

By the time the sixth of our chickens, a panic-stricken candyfloss on legs named Egatha, had been half-eaten alive by squirming parasites, a dead hen had become seemingly just as much a part of our day-to-day rural Nottinghamshire lives as the nearby hum of a combine harvester or the smell of a burning Ford Escort coming from the picnic layby at the top of the hill. Not, of course, that we ever *witnessed* the death itself.

'Finished him off wi' t' shovel,' Frank would say, emerging from behind yet another hedge. Frank was one of those countryside men who called all animals 'him', regardless of their gender. 'Don't have to worry about t' mess. I'll deal wi' it.'

While my dad thanked him and discussed one of the numerous crime waves sweeping our three-building neigh-bourhood – the tying up and beating of the couple at the farmhouse down the track, perhaps, the entirely unrelated armed robbers who'd been hiding out in the adjacent woods, or the hungry fox that Frank had come to view as his arch-rival – Frank would hand me the shovel. I'm not sure quite sure why he handed it to me, but I would take it anyway, just to give myself the illusion that I was contributing.

During our time in Ockwold, I'd got accustomed to laconic men thrusting death-tainted objects into my hand. While home alone, I'd often had to answer the door to the local gamekeeper – a man with a huge bulbous nose and a complexion like rice paper pressed onto offal – and watch dumbfounded as he wordlessly shoved three still-warm, yet emphatically deceased pheasants at me. You might have imagined this would have chipped away at my inborn squeamishness, but I always felt queasy holding an instrument that only seconds previously had brought about the demise of something so fluffy and helpless.

You only had to watch my dad chopping logs or building the chicken run to see he had no trouble throwing himself into country life. Having repeatedly campaigned and petitioned for us to live in the middle of nowhere, he liked to picture himself as a take-care sort of outdoorsman. When it came down to the literal meat and bones of the country, however, he was found wanting.

In the anecdotes my dad told to friends, Frank's mercy killings were always painted more as a favour to Frank from us than one from him to us: naturally my dad *could* have finished off the half-dead rabbit or mouse or stoat, but with Frank standing there behind the hedge, dribbling with anticipation, it hardly seemed fair to deny him.

'DID I TELL YOU HE'S GOT A LITTLE PLATFORM OF EARTH IN HIS BACK GARDEN WHERE HE KILLS THEM?' my dad would say to a pair of enthralled, urban-dwelling NUT workers in our living room. 'HE EVEN SOMETIMES MAKES HIMSELF A CUP OF TEA FIRST AND GETS ONE OF HIS CAMPING CHAIRS OUT.'

The way he portrayed it, by letting our neighbour put our wounded out of their misery, we were doing the community a service: if Frank hadn't been popping up from behind one of our hedges with a rifle in his hand and a bloodthirsty grin on his face, he would have been making a nuisance of himself on Nottinghamshire's public footpaths, looking out for rabbits who'd been incautious with barbed wire fencing and making presumptuous offers to the owners of three-legged dogs. But I knew, my mum knew and he knew that he wasn't telling the whole story. I'd seen my dad on the few occasions when he'd put a small creature out of its misery on his own, and he was the solemn antithesis of a man in his element. One time, shortly after The Slink – a much fiercer predator than her nervously low-slung gait would suggest – had left a mouse to writhe around on the kitchen floor with a broken back, I'd watched through my bedroom window as he placed the unfortunate creature in a Sainsbury's carrier bag and reversed over it in his Vauxhall Astra estate.

Of course, not being on the main household committee, I had the luxury of staying out of matters of animal euthanasia. As someone known to suffer weeks of remorse after accidentally treading on a money spider, I had never for a moment considered taking a mallet or spade to one of the half-dead rodents that Monty and The Slink left on the back doorstep.

Curled up happily on my bed or trotting alongside me in the countryside, Monty was incontrovertibly my cat, but with a paralysed shrew between his teeth, he became my parents' responsibility. If his hunting was getting out of control, well, surely that was because they hadn't been disciplined enough with him or weren't buying him enough cat food. As the people in charge, it fell under their jurisdiction.

Five years later in Norfolk, though, when the disfigurement began in earnest, it was not so easy to wash my hands of the matter.

If there was an interim period between stage one of Brewer's kittenhood, where he seemed to spend 90 per cent of his days climbing up the patio doors and crying at me to let him in out of the cold, and stage two, where he became the East Anglian animal kingdom's answer to Son of Sam, I must have blinked and missed it. His voice might have still been of a tone that made every passing pushchair a potential misunderstanding, but, in purely physical terms, he came out in the spring of 2002 with all guns blazing, ready to put his milksop months firmly behind him.

Lord knows what would have happened if we hadn't robbed him of his crown jewels. Muscular and silky-coated,[5] he was already, at the age of eight months, considerably larger than The Bear, and visibly gaining on Janet by the day. If you look like that in the cat world and you don't hunt, your peers probably start to question your manhood, but did he really have to start in on those lovely baby rabbits that sometimes wandered through the hedge at the bottom of the garden?

It was quite horrifying, and also somewhat breathtaking, to watch – and not just for us, clearly. Shipley and the newly masculine-ish Ralph had their bloodthirsty moments, but most of the time, they preferred to stay on the sidelines while Brewer got stuck in, with the taut stares of goading men at a cock fight. There was no fight to speak of, but it didn't take long before the first cock arrived. That pheasant really didn't know what hit it when it wandered into our garden: as Brewer took it down I was reminded of an unusually overweight and oblivious centre forward being tackled

---

[5] In his time, Brewer had sent some truly frightful, gaseous substances through his digestive system and it was a constant source of speculation for us how tumble-dryer fresh his pelt always remained.

by a savage left back in a Sunday League football match I'd once watched.

Every so often, Dee or I managed to get in quickly and perform a rescue operation before the fatal bite. Baby sparrows were flicked out of jaws and placed in maximum security recovery in a cardboard box in the spare room, complete with breadcrumbs and a small bowl of water. Sometimes, they'd come through it and we'd release them into the churchyard over the road. More often, we'd return to find them keeled over on their side, frozen in a death mask of bewilderment.

'You . . . did . . . this,' a mouse would say to me, as it pulled itself out of a spilt pile of coffee grounds on the kitchen floor with its one remaining leg. 'Y-y-you . . . gave . . . these killers . . . a . . . h-h-home . . . and . . . let . . . them . . . do . . . what . . . they . . . pleased . . . and . . . now . . . y-y-you're . . . not . . . even . . . man . . . enough . . . to . . . end . . . my . . . s-s-suffering.' My remorse was not assuaged by the knowledge that if I put the poor little sucker in an empty tissue box and hid it in the hedge he would probably peg out from a heart attack in ten minutes flat anyway. I was a bad, bad person.

Nothing, however, quite seemed to underline my inherent cowardliness like the episode with the wood pigeon.

Dee and I had reached an agreement about the most problematic forms of cat-related debris: I was in charge of dead and half-dead things, puke was Dee's area, and when it came to improper bowel movements, we both mucked in. Nonetheless, the appearance of Woody – and if this creature was not called something as uninspired as Woody, it was obvious it was wide-eyed and characterful enough to deserve *some* kind of name – demanded a household summit.

'I really think we have to put it out of its misery,' said Dee, and as I surveyed the light-grey catastrophe in front of me, I could only agree. Nonetheless, the fact remained that I'd never put anything out of its misery in my life, with the possible exception of a chicken casserole I made in Home Economics when I was thirteen. I even had the car keys and a Sainsbury's bag out at one point, but Woody kept looking at me in that way that seemed to say that he'd be right as rain just as soon as he could get that wing working again.

I finally decided that the most compassionate course of action was to put him in a cardboard box, close its upper flaps, and leave it behind a bush, in the hope that in, say, an hour or two, he would drift off gently into a blissful, never-ending sleep. Over the next five hours, I made four return visits. Each time, I'd open the box to find his whirlpool eyes looking up at me in a manner that seemed to say, 'Don't worry about me, I'm absolutely *fine* – 'tis but a scratch.'

When I came back the next morning, he'd gone. I began to concoct a theory about him 'just having needed some rest' or being subject to a rescue operation by a crack team from a nearby rookery. 'Nature is amazingly resilient. Maybe he patched himself up in the night,' I told myself, until I saw a chirpy Shipley sitting on the wall outside the kitchen with a grey feather hanging out of his mouth.

There was no Frank figure in Brunton – or at least not one that I would have felt confident in approaching about my problem. I was alone with my conscience and my cleaning fluids. If you got in there early enough, it was possible to avert disaster, but it meant being permanently on your guard, and learning the tricks of the trade. Were Brewer, Shipley or Ralph to arrive through the door with a 'mousetache' draped across his upper lip and a demon glint in his eye, it was absolutely crucial not to grab at him too hastily, least he try to make a snatch at the victim itself, for this could result in a fatal tightening of the jaws. Much better to have a spray gun on hand. A loud clap of the hands worked sometimes, as well, but that necessitated a two-man operation: one to make the noise, the other ready to jump in with nimble hands and an appropriate receptacle if the rodent was subject to a touchline fumble. It must have been a surprise for the six other members of the Brunton Village Book Group when our dissection of *Tender is the Night* was abruptly interrupted by the arrival of Brewer with a shrieking vole between his teeth. Their bewilderment can only have increased when his owners began to follow him around the room applauding his bloodlust.

Founded by Dee and me and Bob Potter and his wife Rosemary, the book group represented a nebulous attempt on our part to integrate with the local community. 'Local community' in this case meant Bob, Rosemary, a lady called Isabelle who was married to a friend I'd made at the golf club down the road ('the road' being twenty-two miles long), a man called Simon who'd once interviewed me for the *Eastern Daily Press*, a couple called Ben and Molly whom we'd met in a record shop in Norwich, and – when she could make the sixty-mile drive from her home in Suffolk – Dee's step-grandma, Chrissie.

We did bravely venture into the village pub once, but it was clear from the way that the local remand centre officers regarded us over their pints that they had mixed feelings about a long-winded discussion of W. G. Sebald's *The Rings of Saturn* being played out next to the dartboard, and we went back to a monthly alternation between our living room and Bob and Rosemary's.

I'd heard all the stories about provincial book groups: the initial honourable intentions to examine exactly how intentional the feminist subtext of Daphne Du Maurier's *Rebecca* is, followed by the inevitable descent into parish newsletter gossip and wife-swapping. Our group couldn't have been more different, but it did undergo its own kind of degeneration. We all loved Kate Atkinson's *Emotionally Weird*, but when Shipley was doing the Dance of the Rushing Endorphins on the rug in front of you, it was all too easy for good intentions to get abandoned.

Given the domestic predilections of its founders and Chrissie's lifelong animal love, the Brunton Village Book Group's descent into the Brunton Village Moggy Appreciation Society wasn't exactly surprising, but I'm sure the more detailed discussions of Shipley's and Buttercup's dietary habits must have come as a shock to some of the other members – particularly Ben and Molly, who seemed a bit too cool and indie for animal talk. Actually, Ben and Molly seemed a bit too cool and indie for book talk, too. I'd sensed their heart wasn't in it the week they'd announced that they'd decided to watch the film version of *The Virgin Suicides* because they 'couldn't be bothered' to read the book, and, after the night Bob interrupted an analysis of the latter half of John Irving's *The Cider House Rules* to show us how he'd taught his Siamese, Boris, to beg for Bombay mix, I knew it was unlikely that we'd be seeing them again.

Their replacement was a serious-looking man called Nick who lived on the outskirts of Norwich, worshipped Thomas Hardy ('only his poetry, though') and wore black drainpipe jeans. For The Bear, who'd made himself scarce at past book group sessions, particularly when a work of comic or middlebrow fiction was under discussion, the attraction was instant. As he leaped boldly into his lap and began to vigorously pad his upper thigh, his gaze never wavered from Nick's floppy fringe. It was difficult to know quite whether to apologise, offer the two of them temporary use of the spare bedroom, or continue pontificating over Rose

Tremain's *Restoration* as if nothing out of the ordinary had happened.

Before long, The Bear was curled up on his new friend's lap in a tightly packed ball. That Nick was the last to leave that night was, I'm sure, down largely to politeness. After two hours, I decided it was time to step in. Novel as it was for Dee and I to see The Bear sit on a human being for that long, Nick's legs had become a worry. People had contracted deep vein thrombosis from less restricted positions than this. As I gently placed him on an adjacent pouffe, The Bear opened one resentful eye, but it was enough for me to get the message that he'd registered the transgression and added it to his bulging file.

Like all extroverted acts from The Bear, however, that was an anomaly. More often than not, book group nights would end with Bob, Rosemary, Dee and me, together with Chrissie, sitting in front of one of our log fires, each with one of our more happy-go-lucky cats sitting on, or near, our lap. If we were over at Bob and Rosemary's, they'd always add a couple of logs to the fire at the end of the evening – 'for Boris and Buttercup, in case they get cold'.

This was inarguably what people refer to with a happy sigh as The Life. Nonetheless, there are plenty of differences between 'The Life' and 'a life' and plenty of practical reasons why the former is not traditionally lived by people in their mid-twenties.

Less than a year before this time, our social existence had revolved around pubs and gig venues and people our own age, many of whom owned guitars. Now it revolved around living rooms and gardens and people old enough to be our grandparents, many of whom owned complex and expensive barbecues. Some of them actually *were* our grand-parents. For every occasion we looked at the situation in a 'cocoa mug is half-full' way, there was at least one more occasion where we could view it as half-empty. We were young! We had escaped the big city's crime and grime and knowing nepotism! We were soulmates who'd never got on better! Our cats could run free! We drove to car boot sales on Sunday mornings and bought cool 1960s chairs! On the other hand . . . We missed our friends and Skoob Books in Holborn and the Phoenix Theatre Bar on Charing Cross Road and juice bars and delicatessen sandwiches! We were cut off from the world, got in each other's way, and got on each other's nerves more than we used to! Those peacocks over the road kept us awake in the early hours of the morning! The last chair we'd bought from a car boot sale had fleas, and now its base was spattered with vole blood!

One post-book group morning in July of our first summer in Norfolk I came downstairs early to prepare breakfast and found the house abnormally empty. I'd long since been strategically coerced into putting out breakfast for the cats before I prepared the human equivalent. Usually, Brewer would be first to arrive, bolting through the cat door and greeting me with a half-purr-half-chirrup noise slightly reminiscent of a football stadium rattle, followed by Shipley, Ralph, Janet and a dawdling The Bear. But now as I whistled, only Janet appeared, batting my leg with a hungry paw.

I waited a couple of moments and whistled again and saw Ralph emerge from a bush in the garden and make his dejected way in the direction of the house. It took a couple of minutes for the normally hyperactive Shipley to follow him in a similarly downbeat fashion. This was odd behaviour from two cats that would usually fight their way across snow, stream or Alsatian-guarded garden at the vaguest rattle of a biscuit box. Perhaps, like me, they were feeling slow and cotton-wool-headed after an unusually deep sleep.

Our cottage was situated only a matter of feet from the village's lone through-road and our bedroom was situated on the road side of the house. As a light sleeper, it would usually only take the slightest screech of tyres or squawk of the peacocks at the old folks' home across the road to wake me up. A 'slight' squawk, however, had, over the last few months, become an unrealistic fantasy: I might as well have been asking for the soothing snap of a grasshopper's wings in downtown Detroit. Who knows which genius first had the thought that it would be a good idea to install the noisiest birds available to man to add to the 'calming' atmosphere of a home for Alzheimer's patients, but over the last few years, their population had grown in a manner inconsistent with Brunton birdlife.

At four o'clock on a spring morning, it could often feel like we had five fancy-feathered versions of the cawing woman from Monty Python's spam sketch sitting on the wall opposite our house.

For Bob Potter, who'd had to put up with their unholy racket and conspicuous excrement for almost a decade, the birds had become something of an obsession. Arriving home one day the previous summer, he'd found one of them dead on the road outside his front gate. Checking to see that nobody was around, he'd dragged the corpse into his store cupboard. That weekend, he'd barbecued it and served it to several members of his extended family. 'Didn't taste bad, actually,' he told me. 'Bit chewy, though.' I couldn't see my retribution manifesting itself in such eccentric behaviour just yet, but it must be said that when I saw Brewer eyeing up one of their plumes in the back garden, I wasn't struck with the same feelings of melancholy that accompanied his other birdwatching.

Was that why I'd slept so well last night? Had Brewer finally taken his Serengeti dress rehearsal to the next level and, in the process, solved our 'little feathery problem' for us? Were he to have had a life coach, I'm sure they would have described peacocks as 'a logical next move' for him. I'd seen him lying in the lane on his back, sizing them up: a gesture that seemed to suggest not just that birds five times his size had been added to his list of potential quarry, but that those shiny, cocksure metal animals that zoomed along the tarmac so blithely had better watch their step, too.

He'd been spending a lot of time over at the old folks' home recently. From my bedroom window I would often see him or The Bear rooting through the bins for leftovers. They were our wanderers and there was nothing I could do but accept it. That acceptance, though, was somehow easier where The Bear was concerned. As far as we knew, the nearest he'd ever come to hurting another living creature was the time that, with a self-conscious look over his shoulder to check that no mocking contemporaries were watching, he'd savagely bitten into the ear of a felt mouse we'd bought him from Pets at Home. The wayward pull of testosterone, meanwhile, had long been out of the question. We knew he fought with other cats, since he'd often return from his little trips covered in bites and scratches, but it was hard to imagine him starting a fight. His nomadism was something mysterious and pressing and spiritual. Brewer's, on the other hand, seemed more like an act of adolescent defiance.

Half an hour had now passed since I'd first whistled, and I still only had three cats in my eyeline. I'd looked in all The Bear's favourite resting places, not to mention those that used to be his favourite resting places that other, less pioneering cats had since co-opted: the gap above the living room ceiling, the gap behind my records, the warm spot behind the kettle on the kitchen work surface.

When not out slaughtering pheasants, Brewer could frequently be found kicking seven shades of crud out of a stuffed toy otter left over from Dee's childhood, but now the otter lay alone on the spare bedroom floor, in need of a bit of patching up, but probably glad of the rest. I was already mentally putting my shoes on, planning my route around the village, and rehearsing the speech I'd give to the neighbours in order to persuade them to let me search their sheds.

It was my mind's habit at such moments to scroll manically through its library of cats-in-danger paraphernalia: an episode of *Inspector Morse* involving a cat being hanged from a tree that had brought a tear to my eye when I was twelve, a newspaper story about illegal fur trafficking, a horrifying picture I'd seen on a placard held by some animal rights protesters outside Tottenham Court Road tube station. Dee had gone a long way to quelling such alarmism, but when the doorbell rang I already knew that something terrible had happened. In fact, that's not true. When the doorbell rang, I sensed deeply, on a level that had nothing to do with irrational pessimism, that something terrible had happened. I *knew* that something terrible had happened when I opened the door and saw the expression on the woman from next door but two's face.

It had all taken place at just after midnight, while we were sleeping our peacock-free sleep. The remand officer claimed that it wasn't his fault and the cat had come out of nowhere, but our neighbour, who'd been standing by the window trying to get her baby back to sleep at the time, had heard the four-by-four and the whinny of its brakes and could tell that it hadn't been keeping to anything remotely resembling the speed limit. She'd roused her kind husband, who'd rushed the cat to the vets, five miles away – the remand officer had left the scene by now, explaining that he was late for work – but it was in vain. She was almost certain, she said, that the cat was one of ours, since she'd seen it in and near our drive.

'It had a white patch on it, just here,' she said, pointing to her chest.

'W-w-was it small, or big?' I asked.

'Sort of big. Or maybe medium-sized. It was hard to see, in the light, and you'd have to ask my husband to be sure, but he's out at work.'

My brain was now no longer my own. In the seconds it had taken to open the door and digest the information, a manic, mystic force had taken its reins: it had become a faster, more impressive organ, using parts of itself that normally lay dormant, but also a more erratic one. It seemed to feel that if it could create a new cat – a cat from far away that it did not care about, that fitted this description, a cat that nobody had ever really loved and wasn't particularly nice – then it could save this situation. When that didn't work, it started frantically processing the information on hand. The quicker it worked, it seemed, the more chance there was of avoiding disaster. 'A white patch? On the bib? Well, that would be Brewer, wouldn't it? But The Bear had a bit of white on his bib as well – just a light dusting of hair, really, but it could be called a distinguishing feature. Brewer had white bits all over his body. If it was him, you wouldn't say he had a white bit on his chest; you'd say he had white bits on his socks and his back and his chest, wouldn't you?' These weren't thoughts; they were sentences spooling across a computer screen gone haywire.

I woke Dee and told her the awful news. We knew The Bear was not invincible, but in that he'd survived the mean streets of south and east London, carbon monoxide poisoning, the hard shoulder of the M23, asthma, allergies, scabs, a hole in the throat, baldness, domestic upheaval and travels to who knew where, it seemed unlikely to us that something as mundane as jaywalking would be his undoing. When I phoned the vet, she told me that the cat that'd been brought in during the early hours of the morning had 'a really amazingly silky coat'. When I related this to Dee, a traumatised look passed between us. The Bear was never short on surprises, but in that instant we were 99 per cent sure which of our cats we had lost.

Lying in the box in the back room of the vets, wrapped in a towel, Brewer did initially seem to look as immaculate as ever, but when I studied him more closely, what I saw was not the face of one of my pets. It was something much more brutal: a mask of animalistic shock. I actually had to take a step back, almost tripping on a cat basket as I did. And at that moment, I experienced a revelation: my memory of seeing Tabs lying at the side of the road when I was twelve was not real. What my mind had done at some point several years ago was create a picture out of what my dad had told me and turn that picture into a memory. The truth was, I had never before seen one of my cats when it was not alive. I had always been protected.

I suppose I'd always expected that this day would arrive, but what I hadn't expected was that when it came, I'd still feel like I *needed* protecting. Somewhere along the line I had begun to believe in another one of the great lies of adult life: the one that said that because you could grow a beard and fell a tree and fill out a mortgage application, you would naturally begin to care less than you used to about small innocent animals that you'd opted to put in your care. It really was a preposterous piece of propaganda, its subtext seemingly being that animals were just elaborate children's toys that you'd grow out of.

'It's an awful thing,' said the sympathetic lady vet. 'It's amazing how often they get hit on the village roads. People think it's the big busy roads where it's most dangerous, but it's not. It's nearly always the young ones, too.' As she said it, I noticed the big dark bags under her eyes.

A person living in the East Anglian countryside could be reduced to a blob of human jelly if he let himself brood over every bit of roadkill he set eyes on, but if I saw a dead cat at the side of the road, the image would always stay with me for days. It was not just the innocence of the creature itself that haunted me, but the knowledge that, as long as it remained uncollected on the verge, there would still be a family out there hoping that little Moopsy or Mr Winks had just gone on a very long walk, and would soon be back.

The tired vet was right. Eight out of ten of these cats had a youthful, skinny muscularity about them that hinted that they were at the make-or-break, loose cannon stage of their adolescence: a stage whose other side one either comes out of as a more circumspect animal, or doesn't come out of at all. It is unlikely, however, that their traffic play extended to actual *sunbathing* in the road, and, with this in mind, it could certainly be said that Brewer lived closer to the edge than most of his peers. Perhaps a near miss would have made him approach the road with more care and wisdom. On the other hand, it might have made him feel even more untouchable than he already did, and urged him on.

In as much as a 'live fast, die young' philosophy can be applied to a cat, he had embodied it. You could see it in his early, savage attacks on Dee's otter, but that was just the start and, perhaps, if he'd lived, there would have been no stopping him. James Dean spent his leisure time driving speedy cars; Brewer, who would have looked absolutely ridiculous at the wheel of a Porsche, chose to spend his sitting on the road in front of them.

Theories of predestination could definitely be applied to his demise. It could also be argued that the birdlife of Brunton might view it a little more phlegmatically than we did. Hell, I had to try to be philosophical, but it wasn't easy. No, this was not the same as experiencing the death of a close relative or friend, but there was powerful, pivotal pain here – I felt it curdling, two or three inches above my stomach. Powerful enough to change the direction of a couple of lives completely? Possibly not. Powerful enough to turn those lives, say, forty or fifty degrees, or shunt them more powerfully down a road they were already considering taking? Certainly. I'd known that power before and as I knelt in the garden with Dee five days after Brewer's death, burying his ashes and feeling the strange illogical extra sadness of knowing we would be soon be leaving them behind permanently, I knew it again.

And what of The Bear? What did he know? Lots of powerful things, surely. Additionally he now knew that the spot at the back of the cupboard behind the vacuum cleaner packaging was a place where someone could get some serious long-term rest without risk of detection.

SIX WAYS IN WHICH I HAVE TRIED AND FAILED
TO HURT MY CATS' FEELINGS

1. Using air quotes and a sarcastic inflection whilst saying one of their names (e.g 'Yeah, like you've got anything remotely intelligent to say on the subject, "*Ralph*"').

2. Attempting to show them that by weeing on the side of my brand new desk/leaving a vole's nose on the step outside the bathroom/breaking an expensive vase with their tail/getting overexuberant while I am cooking with raw meat, they have seriously, and possibly irreparably, hurt *my* feelings (e.g. 'Shipley, that is unacceptable. Quite frankly, I'm upset now, and so is Dee. In fact, we may not even eat dinner at all now, thanks to you. You may think it's okay to claw my leg and yap like an effete terrier now, but what happens one day when you get out into the wide world? Do you think you want to be known as the kind of cat who climbs up people's legs any time he sees some raw meat he fancies? Do you think grown-up people will still like you, after you get a reputation for doing things like that? Hmm? Hmm? What have you got to say for yourself? Now go outside and *think about what you've done*.').

3. Freaking them out by repeatedly rewinding the Sky Plus and replaying noises from nature programmes made by bigger, tougher cats.

4. Attempting to defuse an incident of living room megalomania by referring to painful memories from the out-of-control culprit's childhood ('Fine, The Bear, snub this expensive new luxury cat igloo and wee on the curtain if you want . . . It's not as if I expected anything else from someone who comes from a family rife with incest and grew up in a place like Crawley.')

5. Threatening to video their noisiest bottom-cleaning sessions and post them on YouTube.

6. Getting home from a long journey and being swamped by the whole smelly lot of them, only to blank them and wave to a more interesting, good-looking cat that I have pretended to spot on the other side of the kitchen.

Black Cats and Englishmen

I'm always a bit suspicious when people tell me that the earth's population can be divided into Dog People and Cat People. First, when you put forward an idea like that, you undermine the existence of a huge portion of the natural world. Just because dogs and cats have traditionally proved more adept than their peers at wheedling their way into our domestic lives, that does not necessarily mean that we should accept that they have cornered the market in spirit animals. I'd be the last to deny that, on my travels, I've seen people who bear remarkable physical and behavioural resemblance to everything from an Afghan hound to an overweight Burmese kitten and back, but I've seen plenty of Vole Women and Parrot Men, too. You could fudge the issue, and pretend that somewhere out there there's an unusually sharp-toothed mongrel or beady-eyed moggy to which the latter people are naturally aligned, but wouldn't you just be fudging yourself?

Secondly, when you're making these kinds of generalisations, it's important to be clear. *Do* you mean Dog Person and Cat Person as in spirit animal, or do you mean Dog

Person and Cat Person as in 'really likes dogs' or 'really likes cats'? There is a difference.

Take me, for example. It probably goes without saying by now that the cat is my favourite animal. But I've been told that, on the whole, my own nature is a lot more dog-like. This information comes from reliable sources, many of whom have owned a selection of Border collies, chihuahas, spaniels and terriers for a number of years and have known me long enough to realise that I'm clumsy, occasionally overly trusting, eager-to-please, and frequently in the habit of begging for treats. I have no choice but to believe it, and I'm sure it explains why, over the years, my cats have found it so easy to manipulate me like a big dumb sock puppet. But I'm certain that I have feline qualities, too. I prefer individual sports to team ones, for example. Those closest to me say that when I want something, I tend to *really* want it. I'm also happy to spend time in my own company.

Another of my cat-like aspects is the perverse behaviour to which I'm sometimes prone. I don't think of myself as a difficult or stubborn person, but when I look back at the grander ebb and flow of my life, it is characterised by a pattern of contrary gestures. Hard-won acceptance among the tough kids in the GCSE badlands of north Notting-hamshire is followed by a deliberate, obstinate defection to the side of the geeks. The ethics of a childhood spent in a working-to-middle-class left-wing home among books, records and art are cold-bloodedly abandoned for golf. Golf is abandoned for a stint in a punk rock band (a real puzzler, this one, since the music I tend to like most is precisely the stuff punk came to kill). The isolation of the countryside is abandoned for London. London is abandoned for the coun-tryside. If cats enjoy spending time in company, it's perhaps because they can naturally empathise with such obtuse behaviour.

I certainly wouldn't recommend this style of living as any kind of template for a sane, well-rounded existence, but for the first two and a half decades of my life, it served me quite nicely. I also know that in late 2002, when I felt the pull of my Contrary Gene once again and chose to ignore it and opt for a more moderate approach, things didn't work out quite so well. The six months that followed perhaps go a long way to explaining why cats live a happier life for failing to acknowledge such thorny concepts as 'middle ground' and 'compromise'.

Either that, or they simply illustrate that when you are considering buying a house and you hear thumping techno music coming from the house attached to it at 11 a.m. in the morning and, when you ask the vendor if such music is a problem, they tell you they've 'never heard a thing' and 'the walls are too thick anyway', you should run far, far away.

Dee and I had already been toying with the idea of selling our cottage in Brunton before Brewer's death, but in the days that followed it, as every four-by-four that zoomed by our windows loomed larger than ever in our imagination, the scales were tipped. The mere possibility that, by staying put, we might be putting Ralph, Janet, The Bear and Shipley in danger was horrifying. Add that to our continuing fears about being cut off from society, and our decision was made.

Understandably, a move back to the capital was tabled. Of the fifteen or so friends who'd talked so excitedly about 'following' us to Norfolk in the aftermath of our wedding, only one couple had braved the move. Even more isolated than us and with an even more gargantuan renovation project to suck up their time, they'd split up not long afterwards. The others who did manage to make it up to visit us did their best to pretend not to be underwhelmed by what they found, but we could see their bewilderment. 'I know there must be an Aga here somewhere,' their eyes seemed to say, 'but I'm just not seeing it.' I'm not sure what they were expecting – maybe a cross between an interior shoot from *Country Life* magazine and something that you'd find on the sleeve of an early Fairport Convention album. Whatever it was, it almost certainly didn't involve the Brunton Remand Centre or the area's numerous derelict petrol stations.

But moving back to London would be admitting defeat, wouldn't it? And what kind of life would living in a tiny two-bedroom flat backing onto a communal yard in Greenwich or Putney (borders) constitute for Shipley, Ralph, Janet and The Bear? Besides, it wasn't as if we didn't like living in Norfolk itself: we'd been falling further and further in love with the county's unassuming cheeriness and ruggedly understated landscape for eighteen months now.

We decided to look for a happy medium – the kind of place an estate agent would describe as 'close to local amenities' but which simultaneously touched on rural tranquillity – and Devlin's Cottage, in the town of Holsham, a few miles north of Norwich, fitted the bill. All sixteenth-century beams and crooked, murderous staircases, its situation, on a long row of similar terraces on a one-way street spotted with speed bumps, was such that, providing we were careful whilst opening the front door, the cats would have their work cut out to get to any road in the vicinity, let alone one traversed regularly by speeding Range Rover drivers. Instead, they would have their own little paradise: a tinkling stream at the

bottom of the garden and an adjacent meadow and churchyard.

And us? Well, we'd have a considerably smaller living
space, and we'd miss Bob and Rosemary, but we'd also have
a less formidable mortgage, allowing us to finally fully appreciate our more sedate choice of life. Not having to drive ten
miles every time we ran out of Persil non-bio would be nice,
too.

The noise terrorism began on Christmas Eve, the day
we moved in, and did not let up until the day the following June when we were finally driven out of the place for
good. At first we told ourselves that it was Christmas, and,
while that season was not traditionally associated with
sitting in one's bedroom and playing drum'n'bass at top
volume, we should live and let live. Then, when our other,
slightly cowed, neighbours met us and told us how sorry
they were to find that we had been palmed off with the
cottage adjoining the 'problem house', we told ourselves
that maybe our 19-year-old, wannabe DJ neighbour would
soon get a job or get a place of his own and stop living
with his mum. Much of what happened afterwards belongs
in another, much darker book. Let it suffice to say that
finally, after trying and failing to appeal gently to the DJ
and his browbeaten yet fiercely loyal mum – a woman
who, shortly after first introducing herself on the week
we moved in, greeted us with the phrase 'I saw you out my
window and I said to myself that I could *tell* you weren't
from round here' – and wasting day after day building
cases with the council for a noise abatement order and
with our solicitors against Devlin's Cottage's former
owners, we called it quits and put a deposit on a rented
house just outside Norwich.

To be completely fair, in the week before we moved,

the repetitive beats had been reduced to a level where they didn't quite make our wood burner shake so violently or send the cats running quite so quickly out into garden with their fur standing on end. We *had* experienced a full three weeks of respite since the last time one of the DJ's friends had vomited on our front door, but by then the place had become tainted for us: it had been asking to be renamed from the off, and continuing to refrain from referring to it as Devil's Cottage would have been an act of gross insincerity.

'If you get it wrong, you'll get it right next time,' went the excellent song on the radio in my friend Don's van, the day he helped me pick up the last of our furniture from the house. I could see what the lyrics were getting at, but it seemed to me that 'if you get it wrong, you'll get it wrong the next time as well, and the time after that, but after that you might get it right, if you're lucky' was a more universal maxim. I'd heard the old adages about failures being a necessary part of success but, as someone who had lived in houses with noise problems before, and who came from a family who'd turned property disasters into an artform, I felt that this was one failure I could have avoided. When Michael, the mystically inclined folkie friend who'd so kindly looked after The Bear when we'd first moved to Norfolk, claimed that our bad luck was something to do with the peacock feathers we'd put in a jar – what he called 'the evil eye' – I took it with a pinch of salt, but when I looked back at my life as a house mover it was hard not to feel like the victim of some kind of voodoo.

Dee, too, had done enough househunting in her time to know the warning signs. But the couple who'd sold Devil's Cottage to us had had a Golden retriever, and people with

Golden retrievers didn't lie, did they? If only we'd been able to ask The Bear's opinion, we probably could have saved ourselves a lot of trouble. From the moment he first stepped into the living room, sniffed the carpet, curved his tail violently, and scuttled behind the washing machine, you could tell he didn't like the place.

If I was beginning to feel the stigma of The Guy who Moves House a Lot, I could at least console myself that I wasn't alone. My grand life total of house moves was now sixteen, which was only four more than The Bear's – only two, actually, if you count his relocation to and from the hard shoulder of the M23 – and considering that he was two decades younger than me, you could argue that, of the two of us, he'd had it considerably worse. By now, his Bear sense would tingle at even the most inconclusive glimpse of packaging. If we bought a hairdryer or new computer, we'd make sure we were quick to hide the evidence. He'd always had a love–hate relationship with cardboard, but after our move to Devil's Cottage, this took on an almost sadomasochistic aspect. In his opinion, there were only two things worth doing with a box. If it was there to signal more upheaval in your life, you pissed on it. If it came in peace, you curled up in it. Sometimes, you just said the hell with it and did both at the same time.

If ever there'd been a time when Dee and I genuinely wanted to be granted our wish of being able to talk to our cats, it was now. What we would have given to have been able to sit all four of them down and tell them that all this upheaval was going to be for the best in the long run, and that, even though it might not seem that way sometimes, we had their best interests at heart. I'd seen that 'I'm going to have to be the new kid at school again, aren't I?' look before – in the mirror, among other places – and I was now realising it was by no means exclusive to the human species.

Much as they seemed to like Devil's Cottage's backdrop, it was fairly obvious that none of them had any great affection for the wonky, portentous edifice itself. While not quite of a volume that would combat next door's zombie techno beats, Ralph's witching hour whining had reached an all-time high of piercing insistence. As he wandered the tiny rooms of the building, he would sound like he was reading a list of grievances off a tiny clipboard, ticking them off as he went along. 'Reaarrroow!' Tick! 'Beeeullawgh' Tick! 'Seegraaaeooowgh!' Tick! Janet was never one to wear his darker emotions on his sleeve, but one couldn't help noticing that, when he squatted on The Bear's back, he did not do so with quite the élan of old. While also essentially upbeat, and typically chatty, Shipley had undergone a remarkable physical transformation: the Mohican that he had displayed the first time he heard the bark of the DJ's Great Dane[6] had now frozen permanently to his back like biological armour, primed to expand at the first sign of danger, but never fully deflating.

But it was The Bear, as ever, who proved our major concern. He did his share of hissing and adopted a formidable enough hind-legged pose when Shipley or Janet overstepped the mark, but I'd still never seen him attack another cat, and considered such an occurrence a physical impossibility.

---

[6] Sorry, did I forget to mention the constantly barking Great Dane? I did, didn't I? Still, such a thing can seem a minor aural concern, when you feel like you're trapped inside a giant industrial heartbeat and you're beginning to appreciate just why the repeated playing of Van Halen proved such an effective form of psychological warfare in the smoking out of General Noriega from the Holy See's embassy in Panama.

Yet the cuts on his body when he returned from scoping out Devil's Cottage's surrounding area suggested that he was doing battle with *something*.

His left ear now had an inch-long battle rip starting at its tip, and, while he would have to lose a lot of weight and fur before he once again came to resemble the forlorn creature who'd stolen my chicken bhuna two autumns ago, he was beginning to look a little torn and frayed about his edges. There was a new, rather strange looseness to his under-carriage.

'Och! You're nae to worry about that! He's just got saggy boobies!' exclaimed his latest vet – a very camp, and very Scottish, lady who seemed to be fixing to take him home with her – as she injected his VIP flea treatment. Nonetheless, one only had to see the new wariness to his watchful waddle to realise that he was a cat with a weight on his mind, and convinced that at any moment another, heavier one – possibly in the shape of a cartoon anvil with '10 Tons!' chalked across it – could descend from above.

But what made me the expert? Who's to say that in those moments just before we left Devil's Cottage, when he scut-tled into the living room, looked deep into my eyes, and proceeded to squirt a fountain of steaming fluorescent urine onto the rare books of East Anglian folklore that I had just carefully packed away, he wasn't experiencing a moment of exquisite, untrammelled happiness? Having spent much of my late teens and early twenties with fans of indie rock and maudlin beat literature, I'd met plenty of people who claimed that depression was their own personal, twisted form of happiness, and there was nothing to say that The Bear wasn't their moggy equivalent.

As morose as The Bear was, I could not help but notice that in the six months we spent at Devil's Cottage, I received more frequent affection from him than ever before. At Brunton, I'd never quite cemented the intermittent bond I'd made with him at Blackheath, largely because I'd been too busy dealing with the killing, shitting, wailing twelve-legged typhoon that was Brewer, Shipley and Ralph. But alone in my study on the tiny attic floor of Devil's Cottage – or 'the turret' as I'd begun to think of it – trying to work on my Norfolk ghost novel and shut out the shuddering metronome on the other side of the wall and plan our escape, I'd find myself the subject of a single-minded Bearline. As he jumped on my lap and I ran my hands along his flanks, I'd feel pleasure pulsate through him and he'd begin a tweeting falsetto purr. If I got lucky, this would evolve into a series of gentle nips to my forearm.

He was always easily distracted – as little as a rogue gust of air could do the job, and if I so much as contemplated clearing my throat or sneezing, I could forget it – but part of what made these spells so special was their fragility. Was he healing me? Getting off on my negative energy? Both? It was no wonder that the role of the black cat in folklore was traditionally the cause of such divergent speculation. This one had been crossing my path for almost three years, and I still didn't know what it meant.

Dee sometimes caught the thunderbolt, too. Wandering through the house wearing earplugs, fighting off a migraine and trying to think of a productive activity that would not be interrupted by the 'thud-thud' of idiot cartoon techno, she would hear a 'meeyooooeey' sound, and find The Bear shadowing her steps, with an expectant air about him.

'I'm not sure if he's forgiven me, but I think he might have finally decided he doesn't completely hate me,' she said. She may have spoken too soon, though, since about five minutes later he covertly dribbled wee on a 1960s handbag she'd just sold to a man in Singapore.

'Now, The Bear, why did you want to do that?' she asked gently, picking him up beneath his shoulders.

Had Ralph, Janet or Shipley done the same thing, she would have almost certainly called them a crapweasel or a nobwaffle by now and threatened to fashion them into a replacement for the soiled item, but her tone with The Bear was perennially that of the primary school teacher with the autistic maths prodigy. Eight years they'd been together now, on and off, and she still did not seem to have completely given up on the possibility of him opening up and telling her his deepest thoughts. To give her credit, I thought she might get her wish this time. For just a split second, his mouth opened and it seemed that he was forcing out the first words of a monologue about his troubled childhood, but in the end he just had an asthma attack.

Whatever The Bear's emotional temperature, I felt certain that he'd come to unequivocally love our next house, in the 'city village' of Trowse, on the outskirts of Norwich. At the end of a day of futile, frustrating househunting – how were we ever going to be in a position to buy another house when selling ours was going to be so difficult? – Staithe Cottage had shimmered in front of us like an oasis in the summer heat. Visiting it had been little more than an afterthought. Two hours earlier, the notion of moving into rented accommodation had still been one that we'd not fully thrashed out, but after a single glance at the adjacent river and the enormous living room that stretched out over the water on stilts, a tiny nod passed between us that said our tenancy agreement was already as good as signed.

The picture I'd seen on the Internet of a pretty yet fairly standardised-looking two-bedroom Norfolk flint cottage really didn't do the place justice. Set down a dusty track a hundred yards from the nearest road, together with four houses of complementary style, it was just about the most peaceful spot either of us had ever clapped eyes on, yet it was only half an hour's walk from the centre of Norwich, our favourite city. And all this for only slightly more per month than what I'd paid not all that long ago for a tiny one-room flat in south London.

As the landlord, a gruff, bearded architect called Richard, proudly told us of how he'd found the place in near-derelict condition in the late eighties and lovingly restored and extended it, we popped our heads through the trapdoor in the living room floor and looked down into the depths of the river. Resurfacing, we were surprised to find that we had been joined by the departing tenant. She was rather hairy, and, even by Norfolk standards, her greeting was distinctly on the laid-back side.

'Oh, this is just Tibs,' said Richard, picking her up and smoothing a hand along her arthritic-looking spine and onto her withered tortoiseshell tail. 'My wife and I used to live here ourselves. Now we live next door, but Tibs still likes to use it as her granny flat.'

This was useful information, in that it made my next question, regarding the precise rigidity of that 'no pets' clause in the homogeneous tenancy literature, somewhat less fraught. It soon became obvious that not only we, but our animals too, would be welcome here. We wouldn't even have to use our ever-reliable back-up plan of pretending that we actually only had two cats: Ralph and an unusually chameleonic black phantom who could shrink and expand at will to resemble Janet, Shipley or The Bear.

The day we moved in was one of hottest of the year. After Don had finished helping us unload our furniture from his van and let his black Labrador – Don did slightly resemble a Labrador, now I came to think of it – splash about in the river, we settled down for lunch on the balcony next to it. Our property problems were far from over: already both of us were upping our workload, two-thirds of my beloved collection of rare vinyl was on eBay in order to help us out of our jam, and we knew that being candid about Devil's Cottage to potential buyers was going to mean that it could take a long time to sell, and even then probably at a price significantly less than its market value.

For the moment, however, the 'out of sight, out of mind' rule applied. As we said hello to a passing pair of canoeists and watched Shipley and Janet make their first snuffling forays into the meadow opposite the house, I couldn't help but think of that overused property phrase 'living the dream'. It was not a phrase I liked, partly because if I was really going to live one of my dreams it would probably involve me resitting my GCSEs and realising I hadn't got any pens whilst simultaneously walking through a series of endless doors watched by various friends and former Blue Peter presenters, all of whom would suddenly develop the faces of wolves. Nonetheless, I supposed that when people used that phrase, they were talking about something like the scene before us.

It was such a cliché, and so damn *good* with it, Dee and I couldn't help but chuckle. That said, with hindsight I probably did take my elation a bit too far by jumping in the river, particularly in view of what one of our neighbours told us later about her friend who contracted Weil's disease after doing the same thing.

I knew enough about The Bear now not to second-guess his moods, so when, two days later, he disdainfully licked the butter off his paws and vanished, I wasn't surprised. I had by now developed a theory that with every new place we moved to, he would view it as his duty to walk and walk until he was sure that The Actor's old flat was not some-where in a ten-mile radius.

We had not heard from his former soulmate since his move to Australia two years previously, but The Bear did not know that and, as far as he was concerned, there was nothing not to say that the two of them were not wander-ing the countryside in matching states of emptiness, biding their time by performing unreasonable acts with cardboard until their exalted reunion. Given that a person could not walk more than two miles in any direction without being confronted by one of two rivers, a dual carriageway, a dry ski slope or the Norwich branch of the Big Yellow storage depot, Dee and I reasoned that it would not be long before he decided to turn back, but a week later, when our rea-soning was getting a little shakier, we received an intriguing telephone call from our estate agent, who'd been showing a couple of pensioners around Devil's Cottage.

'How did the viewing go?' I asked her, impressing myself by resisting the temptation to add: 'Please say they wanted to buy it and then I might not have to sell my original copy of Nick Drake's *Five Leaves Left*!'

'I think they liked it, but the husband was a bit worried about how narrow the staircase was,' she said. 'Actually, that's not the reason I'm calling. What I wondered was, when I show the house in future, would you like me to let your cat out, or would you prefer it if I kept him locked inside?'

'I'm sorry. Could you say that again?'

'Your cat. The black one. At least, I assume he's yours. He was sitting in a cardboard box when we went into the upstairs bedroom. He looked very pleased with himself.'

It was his most confounding masterstroke yet. I mean . . . I knew we'd been a bit lenient in letting him out of his carrier on the ten-mile drive from Holsham to Trowse, and he *did* have a look of uniquely intense concentration on his face as he stared out the back window, but this was remarkable. How, we wondered, as we hurried to the car, had he found his bearings, known to take the third exit at the Heartsease roundabout and not the one before it that looks a bit like it, negotiated the A47 bypass?

About half an hour later, we got our answer. You could have said the jet black cat that greeted us so cheerily at the front door of our house of pain looked a bit like The Bear, but probably only if you were extremely short-sighted or the feline equivalent of a racist. I had no idea where this overweight, flirty-tailed creature came from or to whom it belonged, but from the dark glaze of fur covering every carpet, it was obvious that it had been making itself at home. One might have hoped it would have offered us some form of token rent payment by, say, undertaking some pest control in our molehill-strewn garden or – better still – shimmying its ample behind up to the exhaust pipe of next door's Subaru and filling it with a giant turd, but it was clear that there was only one kind of squatting going on here.

'You know that The Bear is probably going to be curled

up on the bed when we get back,' said Dee, after we'd
deposited the cat in the garden and finished taping the cat-
flap up.

She was almost right: the following morning, back in our
lovely rented house, we came downstairs to find him on the
bean bag, sleeping off his bender with an apparent
vengeance. I opted for the nonchalant approach, strolling
straight onto the balcony with my cornflakes without stopping to pet or fuss him, but I'm sure we both knew it was an
act. If he'd been fully conscious – and was that one soulful
eye I saw opening just a crack as I went past? – I'm sure he
would have been able to look at me and see beyond my skin
to the relief that was flooding through me.

It was preposterous to think that he'd been the one
pulling the strings to our emotions for the last twenty-four
hours: the kind of supernatural speculation that even Folk
Michael would have written off as poppycock. Still, there
was nothing to say that, somewhere during our final days
at Devil's Cottage, either as a practical joke or as an
innocent act of generosity, The Bear hadn't tipped off a
dumb, fluffy-tailed friend about the empty house. There
were all sorts of messages being passed between cats all
the time: a hidden, finely nuanced language seething with
miniature power struggles, unfinished business and abiding
vendettas.

With dogs, it just wasn't the same. As we got settled in
Trowse, I started to walk Nouster, Richard the landlord's
Border collie, over to the nearby country park, and I closely
observed his encounters with other members of his species.
The difference between watching these and watching, for
example, Shipley's encounters with Spooky, the big black
tom owned by our neighbour Jenny, was the difference
between watching two boozed-up football hooligans rowdily

greeting each other on the street, and watching two college professors – one of whom had previously slept with the other's wife and given his book a scathing review in an academic journal – size each other up over the crème de menthe at a dinner party.

Even Nouster's relationship with his ultimate nemesis, a darker-hued, permanently chained-up Border collie who lived at the other side of the meadow behind our house and went by the nickname 'Black Fang', had none of the gradations of The Bear's relationship with Janet. And this was *Janet* we were talking about: no cat genius, and certainly not an animal who you'd frequently find yourself using a word like 'gradations' about.

The secret dialogue of cats, the esoteric catiquette that they thrash out and mould between them, is one of the great fascinations and frustrations of owning them. The greater the number you own, the more amplified such fascination and frustration becomes.

What, for example, was currently the beef between Ralph and Shipley? A matter of months ago, they'd still been sleeping together in a classically kittenish 'pile of paws' formation and cleaning one another's ear gunk, but now each regarded the other with caution and the punch-ups, while still brotherly, could get vicious. Did this all stem from the time that I'd given them both a going over with our JML Pet Mitt and Ralph had got just a bit more time than his brother? Did it go back to when Dee bought that extra-strong black market catnip from the online herbalist and Shipley got a bit bug-eyed and greedy?

Or had it all simply started one day when one of them looked at the other one's bird in a funny way? Irritatingly, nobody could tell me, though I sensed that, in Shipley's case, it wasn't for lack of trying. In two years, that little

meeyap had developed into something much more garrulous and strident. Dee loved him, and could still reduce
him to beatific state by spending three minutes deftly
stroking his forehead, but she was the first to confess that
she sometimes found him obnoxious, loud and grasping.
Since both were highly opinionated, particularly on culi-
nary matters, it was inevitable that they would sometimes
lock horns.

'When you're cooking chicken,' I'd hear Dee say to
Shipley, 'do *I* start jumping around and clawing the back of
your legs and singing "The Chicken Song" to *you*?'

'The Chicken Song' wasn't really a song about chickens
any more than Genesis's 'The Lamb Lies Down on Broadway' was a song about a lamb lying down on Broadway. It
was really more of an abstract a cappella number Shipley
sometimes liked to toy around with upon being confronted
with raw poultry. It drove Dee mad, and she viewed it as one
might the antics of a particularly tiresome office joker, but I
always had an impulse to applaud every time it started up.

I swelled with pride at the assertiveness and increasingly
impressive physical presence of the runt I told myself I'd
rescued from Romford obscurity. The understanding was
that Shipley was ultimately my cat, in much the same way
as Ralph was ultimately Dee's cat. And, as Shipley's
supreme guardian, I enjoyed hearing such varying reports
on his day as 'Ekwwwekaarapplle!' ('It's bloody raining out
there again – please dry my paws off with a tissue immediately!') and 'Eeeymeewikiwikeeyapeeeymekweeeekeyap!'
('IwentoutsideandtherewasagooseitmadeanoiseatmeIcan'te
atitliketheotherflyingmice'). When I was too busy to pay
full attention to his news, he usually resorted to more
extreme measures, tearing with his front teeth into whatever document happened to be lying on my desk with no

regard for its bearing on the following month's household income.

On one occasion, when I'd ignored an overlong anecdote he was trying to tell me about the biscuit dispenser being empty and callously nipped off to get a cup of tea, he laid devastating waste to a short ghost story I'd been trying to write about a man who lives by a river and walks his neighbour's dog. I suppose it was his way of telling me that the dialogue was cloth-eared, the non-autobiographical elements didn't ring true and my narrative voice was woefully undeveloped. If so, as a piece of literary criticism, it was both incisive and exacting. I can only think that when, a month or so later, during one of his ritual *Daily Mirror*-chewing sessions, he ripped the word 'pants' out of the paper and dropped it at my feet, he was offering a postscript.

A time that I was particularly glad of Shipley's word-smithery was in January 2004, when he managed to smuggle his way into our local mail van. The postman – a gentle man called Dave, with a strong Norfolk accent and a habit of inviting himself into my living room to soliloquise on the early albums of Deep Purple – had got almost a mile down the road towards Norwich before he heard the yapping coming from behind his seat. His first thought was that Jenny-from-across-the-track's terrier-spaniel cross, a beautiful little piglet of a dog called Tansy, had stowed away in there. Turning round and seeing the sharp, inquisitive features of a sinewy black cat was a momentary heart-stopper, but Dave said he wasn't really all that surprised, and neither were we. Shipley had always had a soft spot for members of the delivery trade.

'He's been after me parcels for months now,' said Dave. 'I've already shooed him out of here twice this week. Good job he's got a loud voice. These diesel engines aren't exactly quiet.' From what I could work out from Dave's retelling, the noise Shipley had made had held no terror or apprehension. It was more of a polite, overexcited enquiry regarding the destination of their little adventure together and whether, when they got there, there would be any chicken-flavoured snacks available.

I'd known from very early on that Shipley had some serious cattitude. He did not have Ralph's ruffled beauty, or The Bear's cunning, or Janet's ability to take the good with the bad, but when it came to pure energy, he outshone them all. Keen to make the most of my new, rambling-friendly habitat, and taking note of his hound-like qualities and fondness for travel, it was perhaps only logical that my thoughts would turn back to Monty, and I would invite Shipley on a walk with me through the meadow across from the house. I wouldn't have insulted The Bear's intelligence by proposing that he joined in with such a flippant activity, and by that point he was far too busy with his new obsession: climbing onto the roof of the converted stable where Richard the landlord and his wife Kath lived, pressing his face against the skylight, and staring longingly down at them. Janet was also absent – probably busy trying to befriend a fox. However, not wanting to show favouritism, I invited Ralph to join us.

To be frank, I didn't have high hopes for Ralph's capabilities as a power-walker. This was not just because I was worried that the remotest brush with a Shetland pony or Jack Russell could result in one of his prolonged whining sessions. Since Brewer's death, he seemed to feel, in killing terms, that he had some kind of obligation to take up where his brother left off. Fortunately, his homicide had not yet become excessive, nor had it confirmed some ominous thoughts I'd had after finding out Staithe Cottage's original incarnation had been as a staithe where local meat traders would hang their carcasses to cool.

Lately, however, he'd been taking a more than passing interest in the two swans who circled the living room every morning, waiting for my toast crusts. The whole thing was obviously a misunderstanding. From where Ralph sat on the riverbank, two-thirds of the swans' bodies remained obscured by the water or the stone ledge leading down to the river. That still made them big birds, but not nearly as big as they actually were, and Ralph – his memory of Brewer and the pheasant presumably undimmed – must have frequently told himself he could take them, no sweat (see below). Sure enough, before we'd reached the stile at the

end of the track leading to the meadow, he'd scuttled off in the direction of the river, having spotted a bright white wing in his peripheral vision.

Shipley managed another 500 yards and seemed enthusiastic, but turned back after hearing some raucous teenagers boating on the broad on the other side of the field. As I saw his raised Mohican recede into the distance, I could hear him soundtracking every hurried step of his journey back to the cat-flap. I told Dee later that I was sure that, in between the meeyaps, I'd heard the phrase 'I'moutofheretogetsomechicken', but I probably imagined it. As she very rationally pointed out, 'I'm sure when you have a repertoire of noises as eclectic as that, the law of chance says you're bound to come out with the odd proper word every now and again.'

Seeing my disappointment, she went straight to her computer search engine, with the help of which she managed to track down a cat lead. What she was proposing seemed ambitious, but I decided to roll with it, remembering a childhood image of a brace of Siamese strolling imperially around a campsite alongside their owners. Dee had long argued that Shipley had a bit of pedigree in him. True as this might have been, it turned out that it was not the specific bit of pedigree that makes a cat predisposed to relinquishing its independence and agreeing to be treated like a toy fox terrier. You might have imagined he would have mistaken the lead for an unusually stretchy collar, but we hadn't even pulled on it, and his Mohican was already up higher than ever, telling us that it would be unwise to take the experiment any further.

Chastened, I returned to my routine with Nouster, Richard and Kath's dog: a circuit of the nearby broads and the country park, up the hill past Whitlingham Hall, down through the woods, then back through the meadow, where

Nouster would round things up with a ten-minute woozle (named by Richard and Kath, this downright confounding activity involved Nouster watching the ground intently with a raised paw then pouncing on invisible creatures scurrying about far beneath the earth).

I made sure our yomping was completed before dusk, since that was when the country park – like any patch of countryside unusually close to a city centre with a public right of way – began to quickly take on a less salubrious character. Away swam the swans, home went the cyclists and hale and hearty sexagenarian couples with Labradors, and in came the prostitutes, drug dealers and adulterers. In fact, you could say that Whitlingham Park had a rare distinction in that it was not only the regional hot spot for dogging but also the regional hot spot for, well . . . *dogging*. However, I imagine if I had the tough, unquestioning mind of a true Dog Man I would have been less liable to let such notoriety bother me.

Being able to borrow your neighbour's dog at a moment's notice on a 365 day per year basis is a terrific arrangement. You get fresh air and the glowing feeling of an animal's respect, without the hassle of having to hose the muddy broad water off him afterwards and put up with his needy, fetid, baited breath as he eagerly waits until your next sojourn, his mind unable to focus on anything else.

If Nouster had been The Bear, he would have been able to suss me out in seconds flat. One look at me nervously holding onto a bit of rope the time that Richard had asked me to help him moor his sailboat would have told him he was face-to-face with a faker. If that didn't do it, one sniff of my odour – surely so different from the one of pipe smoke, outdoor grind and linseed oil that lingered permanently around his true master – should have given him all the information he needed to know. But, the way Nouster saw it, from the moment I got hold of his choke chain, I was the closest thing to God.

I liked the ego boost that this gave me, but what kind of person would one become, if that sort of behaviour started permeating their expectations elsewhere in their daily existence? A dog might be for life and not just for Christmas, but it serves as a much better primer for the latter than the former. The Bear might not have used those unfathomable North Sea eyes of his to inform me that I was brilliant and clever because I could throw a stick or a squeaky rubber bee for him to chase, and shout 'Keep in!' when a car was coming, but at least I could not accuse him of ever having raised my expectations unrealistically. He would never have led me to believe that life was a walk in a country park where people did what you said when you barked instructions at them and, even if he had, he would have been careful to convey that that park was an equal mixture of light and dark, good and evil.

Like all cats, The Bear knew about nuance and subtlety and grey areas and indecision: I could see it all in his tail every time he moved, and numerous times when he didn't. But sometimes it seemed that his wisdom was even more refined than that of the rest of his species. If I studied Janet or Ralph or Shipley, I would have been required to severely stretch my metaphors to conclude that life was about whining in echoey rooms or having your dignity removed in a neck harness or underestimating the size of waterfowl. What I learned from The Bear, by contrast, was that life was about going from home to home without really meaning or wanting to and not quite knowing if you loved it or hated it, that it was about trying to keep your head above water and fending off illness, that it was about ambivalence, that it was about an eternal search – and not one that would end with a lovely cottage by the river that, sadly, you could never own outright – for something that was unattainable, that it was about pressing your snotty nose against the glass of the skylight. If I ignored the bit about the snot, the echoes were obvious. There really was no getting away from it. The two of us had a lot more in common than I'd once imagined – and quite a bit more than I would have liked to admit.

SOME RANDOM SELECTIONS FROM
THE CAT DICTIONARY: PART III

Bleatpuppy

Derisive term for a cat who is unable to land on any surface without announcing his or her athletic prowess to the world with a small squeak or pip of self-delight.

Ficklespee

The peculiar, tickly sensation experienced whilst swallowing a particularly meaty and recalcitrant bluebottle.

Fool's bogeys

Crunchy yet slightly moist snacks that are passed off as a 'treat' because they cost more and come in smaller, very slightly more lavish packaging, but essentially taste just like other more ostenstibly run-of-the-mill crunchy yet slightly moist snacks.

Mummyfur

Feeling a bit low? Looking back wistfully to that time all those years ago, when you still had testicles, and you could actually remember who your parents were? Why not stretch your claws, find some mummyfur, and get stuck in? Pretty much any soft, non-shiny, recently laundered surface will do, but slightly damp towels and sheepskin are considered the ultimate delicacies of the mummyfur genre.

Simulslurp

The mystic force that, without the need for discussion or consensus, will cause numerous cats in the same room all to clean their most hard-to-get regions at exactly the same time.

Sleeping with the fishes

The particularly contented, lengthy state of REM that occurs after one has clandestinely intercepted one's owners' shopping bags in the wake of their last trip to the seafood counter.

Sucking the nettle

To lick one's tongue with distaste in the aftermath of an unpleasant or demeaning experience (e.g. a meal not to one's liking, or a cuddle from an overbearing child).

Twhisker

Or, alternatively, a 'half-whisker'. Frequently displayed by feral cats who have been caught in traps by sadistic farmers and cat rescue officers, or in the clutches of bigger, scarier ferals ('I was just a twhisker away from twatting that big-tailed ginger plonker'). Sometimes, twiskers grow back, sometimes they don't. Professors of Catology remain in the dark as to exactly why this is. Often mistakenly thought of as a sign of masculinity or 'streetness', the twisker ultimately signifies little aside from bad balance and potential under-mog status.

El Gato Muy Loco

'Are you sure you're doing the right thing?'

'Yeah. It'll be fine.'

'RGGGAAAEEOWW!'

'What about the neighbours?'

'RGGGAAAEEOWW!'

'They seem fine.'

'And you say it's detached?'

'Yes.'

'RGGGAAAEEOWW!'

'Are you sure?'

'No. Actually, during the three times we've been to view it, I've never quite got round to looking at the sides of the building to see if there's another house stuck to them. Of *course* I'm sure.'

'But I thought you wanted to be in the country and it didn't work out when you were in a town. I thought you moved out of London because you wanted to be in the country.'

'RGGGAAAEEOWW!'

'Well, this isn't really in a town. It's hard to explain. It's weird.'

'Sounds *very* weird.'

'RGGGAAAEEOWW!'

'It's great. A total blank canvas. We love it!'

'What about noise?'

'RGGGAAAEEOWW!'

'You can barely hear a thing – not even the road outside.'

'Damp?'

'RGGGAAAEEOWW!'

'None.'

'Dry rot?'

'RGGGAAAEEOWW!'

'Nope, nothing. God, this is hurting my head.'

'Carpets?'

'RGGGAAAEEOWW!'

'Well, they're in a state, but we'll be replacing them.'

'So why hasn't it sold, then? Sounds a bit suspicious to me.'

'RGGGAAAEEOWW! RGGGAAAEEOWW!'

'*Mum.*'

'RGGGAAAEEOWW!'

'Oh, shut up!'

'Thanks.'

'No, not you.'

The longer I lived in rural and semi-rural areas, the more I realised that there were plenty of things I didn't miss about my brief spell as a footloose, irresponsible urbanite living in ignorance of the housing market. Ear infections, stone-hearted landlords, broken central heating systems owned by stone-hearted landlords, chronic hangovers and the estate agent's intern who stole half my deposit on my first flat would all have been right up there somewhere in the top ten. Nonetheless, there were occasions – and they were brief occasions, admittedly, occasions that quickly popped and evaporated into the air like soap bubbles – when I felt I would have welcomed them back like old friends, just to be granted the wish of going back to a more innocent time. Actually, the time wouldn't even have to be all that innocent, just as long as it didn't necessitate me having conversations with my mum about buying and selling houses. It wasn't as if I couldn't see where the lady was coming from.

I've never met anybody for whom moving is a greater issue than it is for my parents. When I was a kid, on the wall of our many houses hung an illustration, etched by my dad, of a goat craning its neck through a fence to munch on the turf of an adjacent field. In its margin, my dad had written the phrase, 'The grass is always greener.' Much as I admire the craftsmanship of this etching, it's hard not to think of it as a kind of inverted voodoo symbol: if you didn't harm it, bad things happened to the person directly associated with it. I didn't pay it too much attention at the time, but in the years since, I've often wondered if my dad ever noticed its pulsing irony as he transported my mum and me around the north-east Midlands, looking for a bucolic utopia where he could paint, write, and leave behind his council estate past and the misery of supply teaching at Nottingham's less reputable secondary schools.

My dad made some bad moves back then and he's the first to admit it, but few of them were anything like the luck that went with them. Looking back at a nine-year period, beginning in 1985, which took in – among other things – a subsiding semi, the sale of an elegant Edwardian villa at the most unwise moment in twentieth-century UK property history, some meddlesome open cast mining, the discovery of a malignant melanoma in one of my mum's retinas and the unearthing of a mine shaft in a back garden, it strikes me that a person could probably repeatedly drive a bulldozer into one's own house and come away in better shape.

If you've been through an experience like that, it's only natural to want to pass on what you've learned to those closest to you. My parents are settled in a house they love now, and their housing market disasters have bonded them in shared wisdom. But while my dad's advice on the subject broadly involves telling me to watch out for nutters or announcing 'MOST STRESSFUL THING IN THE WORLD, MOVING HOUSE!' as he watches Dee and me struggle to get a mattress through a doorway, my mum can now consider herself the hard-bitten owner of a set of property antennae. She knows all the warning signs, and she knows that the old aphorism about life being what happens while you're making other plans never rings truer than when you're moving house.

Nonetheless, when I spoke to her about moving from Trowse to the town of East Mendleham, in south Norfolk, in the summer of 2004, I could sometimes start to feel like the offspring of reformed alcoholics who thought they'd caught him red-handed in necking his first full bottle of Jack Daniels when in reality he'd only been examining the label. Daisy's voluble contributions to these discussions did little to lower the stress level.

My last remaining childhood cat had always been jumpy, but, since she'd crossed the threshold into old age, her eccentricities had hardened into something more unique. For my mum, who still hoped that one day The Slink might become like other cats and decide to purr when she was happy, as opposed to when she was livid, this was a daily source of frustration.

My mum had tried pretty much everything over the years: prawns, pilchards, a dozen different types of brushes, a selection of hand-woven cushions, those expensive brands of cat food that have the adverts with the women in silk dressing gowns who look poised to get down on all fours and tuck in to the meaty goodness themselves . . . None of it had worked in any lasting way, and any minor progress would always be swiftly nullified by my dad who, perhaps in tribute to his favourite ever pet, had taken Monty's old mantle as The Slink's tormentor and made it very much his own.

'HEY? WHAT DID YOU SAY? ARE YOU TALKING ABOUT THAT CAT?' my dad would say, picking up the other receiver, after overhearing my mum tell me about The Slink's latest psychotic purring fit. 'BLOOMIN' THING'S DRIVING ME CRAZY.'

When you're a small, bony tortoiseshell cat with nerve problems and an overactive thyroid, it cannot be easy to co-exist alongside one of the six loudest men in northern Britain. When that person is not particularly fond of you, it must be harder still.

Never let it be said that my dad is not an animal lover, but his taste tends to run to the wild rather than the domestic. We're talking here about a man who has been known to spend a whole afternoon sketching a goat's chin hair, a man who once got so involved in looking at a bull in a field by the side of the road that he drove his Morris Marina into a ditch and had to get the AA to winch it out. But when he is faced with the more high-maintenance members of the natural world, talk quickly becomes cheap and time tight. This perhaps explains why Monty's sturdy self-reliance was so appealing to him, and why The Slink has never been able to come remotely close to living up to it.

He never exactly shared her worldview in the first place,

but since I'd left home, the battle lines had been much more clearly drawn. What my dad failed to see, however, was that every time he stomped down the stairs, colourfully and loudly assassinated The Slink's character or firmly removed her from his favourite armchair, he was only exacerbating his problem. As he upped the volume of his attacks, she upped the volume of her schizophrenia.

By the time of The Slink's thirteenth summer, none of the one- and two-syllable letter formations traditionally employed to suggest cat sounds could any longer be used to evoke the noise that came out of her mouth. Even 'RGGGAAAEEOWW!' is a mere hint of the true gargling horror of it. As the owner of two unusually vocal cats, I knew what it was like to have a large portion of your daily conversations interrupted by cacophonous gibberish, but we were talking about something from another realm entirely here. There truly was no more delicate way of putting it: when I'd read Stephen King's *Pet Sematary*, and the main character's cat had come back from the dead, this was the noise I had imagined it had made.

My mum's theory regarding The Slink's habit of joining in with her phone conversations was rational enough. The Slink, she claimed, had made the quite obvious mistake of thinking that my mum was talking to her, rather than to the banana-shaped plastic thing with the buttons on it in the corner of the room. This didn't, however, explain why, on the occasions when my mum *did* want to talk to The Slink, The Slink remained frustratingly mute, or retreated under a table to purr spitefully.

Now, with the new levels of amplification, the most elementary of my mum's phone calls to a colleague or plumber had the potential for a myriad of mix-ups ('No, there's nothing blocked in the waste disposal, it's fine; that's just my cat!

What? No, my *cat's* not blocked in the waste disposal; she's very happy . . . Oh yes, I'm sure; I can tell because she just spat at me'). Knowing The Slink's habits, I had long since worked out how to circumvent such misunderstandings, but her howling sessions infused my mum's endless worries about my low-level nomadic lifestyle with an extra serum of negativity. If she'd employed a shrunken, demented elderly relative to sit in the background and wail 'Doom!' every time she voiced one of her concerns, the effect could not have been more extreme. When, as a finishing touch, my dad made his customary contribution of bellowing "EY? WHAT DID HE SAY, JO?' and 'TELL HIM TO WATCH OUT FOR NUTTERS!' from a semi-adjacent room, the three-way assault often became a little overwhelming.

It didn't require a therapist to deduce that my parents were worrying about the ways in which the removal vans and change of address stationery of my childhood had left their marks on my adult psyche: was I, like my dad and his goat, fated to have a long, troubled search for that ever-elusive greener grass? Admittedly, moving house had dominated my life for the last few years, and I'd not always made the best decisions. After paying rent in Trowse, mounting an expensive legal campaign against Devil's Cottage's former owners and taking fifteen months to make an honest sale of the place, property had hammered our bank account, leaving me taking on twice as much freelance journalism as I'd ever taken on in the past, and Dee adding more and more of our possessions to her eBay stock.

The beautiful rented house had been our saviour, but in the end it was more property, and property had made us harried and scrabbling. I could admit all that. But if it was lack of caution on which my mum and dad were dwelling, I felt their fears were superfluous, caution being one of the fundamental byproducts of having someone tell you to watch out for nutters at least once a week for the previous two decades. If, meanwhile, they sensed that history was starting to repeat itself, I could immediately point out a couple of obvious holes in their argument.

First, as much as some of my recent moves had been characterised by escape, I *liked* househunting. I liked the manner in which a would-be home could spark the imagination, I liked the sense of possibility offered by twenty minutes surfing on rightmove.co.uk. Moreover, I was married to someone who salivated at the prospect of refurbishing houses. The way the two of us saw it, we were only going to be on the planet for – if we were fortunate – seven or eight decades, and, unless our enthusiasm for cat ownership mysteriously dissipated, we probably weren't going to be spending much of that time going on holiday to lots of different places, so why not spend it living in lots of different places, and getting the satisfaction of reshaping them in the process?

Secondly, when my dad had been searching for his perfect house, his primary objective had always been to find a place that was peaceful, secluded and ultra-countrified. By the time I'd been in Norfolk for three years, my primary objective was markedly different. When you boiled it right down, I wanted to find a place where my cats would be happy and safe.

When Dee and I pulled up next to a 'For Sale' sign, the first question we always asked each other, upon appraising the building beyond it, was, 'How do you think it will suit the pusses?' When you properly thought about it, there were a lot of domiciles out there that simply weren't all that cat-friendly. Flats weren't great, obviously, unless they were on the ground floor and had their own garden. Inner city places on main roads were a complete no-no. As for 'sleepy' village lanes, we'd witnessed the problems of those only too acutely. Houses abutting small country roads were better, but then there was the problem that the cars that came down them usually did so at high speeds, and not with enough frequency for an imprudent moggy not to become gung-ho. The cottage in Trowse had been a better set-up, but during those moments when my anti-nutter training was in overdrive, I couldn't quite convince myself that The Bear's trips up the track and over the lane wouldn't end up with him being run over by a member of the Norwich and District Association of Master Doggers, late for a crucial meeting.

Clearly, you couldn't have it every way you wanted it, but the Upside Down House seemed considerably better than a compromise. Situated on the outskirts of the market town of East Mendleham, it looked, from the road, a bit like a military bunker that someone had managed to half-build before finding out that war had been cancelled and doing their best to turn it into a bungalow instead. As a result of this, the pensioners selling it had received no end of last-minute cancellations from would-be viewers and the house had remained on the market for more than a year. The fact that this couple had also presented the place as having three studies and only one bedroom probably hadn't helped, either.

Anyone with a modicum of imagination, though, would have been able to see the place's potential, particularly by the time they reached the bottom two floors and saw the floor-to-ceiling windows that overlooked the three-acre lake at the bottom of the garden. The Upside Down House reminded me of a human head: yes, it was nondescript at the back, but its front was expressive, and its eyes were on the action.

We'd been there for ten minutes and Dee had already knocked down about four walls in her head and restored the edifice to its 1962 glory, and it wasn't long before I was right there with her. The fact that the Upside Down House was built into one of Norfolk's steepest hills gave its two lower floors a quiet, cave-like feeling, making it hard to believe that a busy B road was only a matter of feet away. It also meant that, should four wingless creatures of the foot-high variety find their curiosity aroused and want to get to the road in question, they would have their work cut out. Provided we were strict about keeping the front door closed, getting to the tarmac would, for them, require either a forty-foot climb up a wall or a spiral staircase and a four-foot jump over a fence, or a circuitous walk of 500 yards. This would take them perilously close to the guffawing men of the local Conservative Club, a pub with a tendency to host bad David Bowie tribute bands, and a gaggle of geese who had developed a reputation for not suffering fools gladly. Even if Ralph, Janet, The Bear or Shipley did venture over the road, they'd find little of interest, other than a branch of Kwik Fit and a 1980s housing estate: surely no match for the layered wilderness of the lake and its surrounding hillside.

Another deciding factor in the move was that water. I didn't feel I'd made the most of the river at Trowse, but I'd been swayed by its suggestion of an easier, more calmly flowing life. As much as my conscience was troubled by knowing I was responsible for introducing four predatory mouths to areas with large populations of birdlife, I liked that the cats liked the water too. Sitting with Shipley or Janet on the balcony, I'd loved watching the way the river could change personality so quickly, from crystal clear, to filmy-scummy, to opaque, to downright muddy. I'd have to say goodbye to that fluctuation. I'd also probably have to say goodbye to the kingfishers and swans and pikes that went with it, since the lake next to the Upside Down House was situated within view of three different supermarket logos and seemed to contain as many empty Stella Artois cans as it did fish.

But a natural expanse of water was a natural expanse of water, and a person couldn't afford to be fussy. That this new expanse would be situated a couple of hundred feet from our house, rather than beneath it, was also not necessarily a negative thing, if one considered the leisure habits of certain more witless felines and the terrifying moment the previous January when I'd had to spectacularly lunge to save Folk Michael from an icy fate after he'd stepped through a sliding door onto what he wrongly thought was a balcony for a 'mystic moment'.

As it turned out, I could hardly have been more wrong about the wildlife in East Mendleham.

Back at Trowse, Richard and Kath had held a long-running competition among tenants and neighbours to be the first to spot an otter in or around the river, for which the prize was several litres of Richard's home-made ale. In almost two decades, nobody had come forward to claim a sighting, and, having tasted the ale in question, I felt certain this was not owing to chicanery on the tenants' or neighbours' part. By contrast, we'd barely paid our conveyancing fees at the Upside Down House when I saw one poke its snout out of the lake, ten feet from the shore. It almost headbutted a Budweiser can on its way up, but didn't seem overly concerned by this, nor by my presence a matter of feet away. Judging by its laid-back attitude, perhaps there was more to be read into its proximity to the can than I'd first imagined.

A few weeks later, I got the fright of my life when I was getting the lawnmower out of the shed and a deer leaped out of the hedge, made a failed attempt to get through the fence into next door's garden, then waded into the water, swam about fifty yards, and cantered away up the hillside towards the town.

I'd like to say that by the time the turtle turned up, I was getting a bit blasé. But whether an Englishman's back garden is beginning to resemble his own mini safari park or not, it's never going to be easy for him to react with a world-weary air when he takes a breather from writing a newspaper review of that week's episode of *Top Gear*, strolls down to the end of the garden and finds himself confronted by an LP-record-sized shell with a little slimy head poking out of it.

Sunning itself on our rotting jetty, this alien presence caught the attention of Shipley and The Bear too, who were mooching around in some nearby reeds at the time. I'd come to expect Shipley to be by far the bolder of the two, but after making one tentative step behind me onto the crumbling wood, he scarpered back towards the house in a chattering, Mohican-led panic, leaving The Bear as my sole backup. I can't quite say what the pair of us were planning to do once we got within shell-shining distance of the turtle, but, if I was completely up front with myself, I was secretly hoping that The Bear had a better idea than I did.

We got about two yards away before it plopped back down into the lake and swam serenely away. I turned back to The Bear and shrugged, but he seemed reluctant to retreat, as if what he was really expecting was for me to take off my trainers and dive in after it. I could only surmise that he felt a kinship with its wise, wisened demeanour and card-carrying loner status.

Considering that turtles aren't indigenous to Norfolk, the obvious conclusion to draw about our new friend was that it was an unwanted household pet, abandoned long ago. It appeared to be surviving okay on the lake's plentiful supply of sticklebacks and lager dregs and the mouldy bread that East Mendleham's notoriously fussy ducks left behind, but as I thought in more detail about its life, a cloud of melancholy descended. What was its sex life like? What did it do for conversation? After entertaining a few fantasies of rescuing it, or at least finding it a mate, I put it out of my mind until about a fortnight later, when I looked out of the window and noticed a strange shape next to the jetty.

At first, I mistook the shape for a heron that sometimes visited the same area. I'm a touch short-sighted, and from the living room window I thought I could make out a torso-shaped blob with something thinner underneath, which I took to be the bird's legs. I was on deadline with another piece of writing at the time, so it wasn't until three or four hours later that I looked out again and noticed it was still there. I had to get almost all the way to the bottom of the garden before I realised that what I'd took to be a torso was a shell, and what I'd assumed was a pair of legs was actually a turtle's head and neck.

As soon as I saw its leg trapped in the wire mesh on top of the jetty I thought it was dead, and not just in a cut-off circulation way, but as I arrived on the wood, the leg twitched. By this point I'd gone into panic mode and all kinds of irrational thoughts were skating through my head, such as 'What if its shell falls off and it turns into Britain's biggest slug?' It was my habit at times like this to turn to Dee, who would be sure to offer a practical solution to the situation, but, having just passed her driving test, she was out enjoying her new automotive freedom, so I switched to my backup plan of getting some kitchen roll. It was a slightly sketchy plan. Nevertheless, it was one I'd come to rely on in the last three years, upon encountering wild animals. I now recalled the phrase 'snapping turtles' and a story my dad had once told me about someone he'd known as a kid who – for some reason I'd long since forgotten – had to have his leg amputated after stroking a terrapin, but the apprehension in me that this created was no excuse for the truly pathetic exercise in limb-flicking that followed.

The turtle was now slowly blinking in that same way wise, aged reptilian extraterrestrials do in sci-fi films thirty seconds before they die. Gathering my senses, I hurried back indoors, discarded the kitchen roll, picked up an old pair of scissors, came back outside and carefully cut the mesh, freeing the leg and allowing the turtle to drop into the water. A moment later, I saw it re-emerge on the other side of the jetty, swimming smoothly out towards the centre of the lake. As I walked back up to the house, I saw The Bear come out from behind our pampas grass and do one of his effeminate, there's-a-demon-on-my-tail runs in the direction of the cat-flap. Was this intended to serve as some form of commentary on the events that had just transpired? Perhaps. On the other hand, it could have just been that time of the afternoon.

Since our move, The Bear had become more visible than I'd ever known him to be. In our three previous houses, his favourite sleeping places were invariably cupboards, boxes, hidey-holes or deep, dark parts of the building known only to him and about 400 woodlice, but now he could often be seen curled up on the second-to-top stair leading to the Upside Down House's kitchen or the wicker footstool next to our book shelves. One only had to witness the care he took settling down in these spots – that third-to-top stair just didn't have the same cachet, and woe betide me if I gently moved the footstool eight inches to the left so I could get at a paperback – to realise that 'location, location, location' was one of his all-important mantras.

Noting that he'd only relieved himself on cardboard boxes two or three times, rather than the usual two or three dozen times, I took his new higher profile as a sure sign that he'd given the house his stamp of approval. While still a little bald around the eyes, his fur had steadily improved in the last year, and as far as I knew, his wanderlust had yet to take him further than next door's garden.

His affection was still capricious, but he had permitted me to add a new move to my repertoire of strokes, which Dee had termed 'Glove Puppet'. This involved him rolling half onto his back, and allowing me to place a hand on his still semi-hairless chest and gently rub it, causing him to fold his front paws over and curl up like a happy prawn. It was an uncharacteristically vulnerable position for a furry elder statesman to put himself in, and I considered my exposure to it an immense privilege.

If the Upside Down House had cast a positive spell on him, I could see why. Standing in the part of its garden from which the Tesco and Kwik Fit logos weren't visible, it was possible to convince yourself that you were in the ultimate rural cat paradise. Add our garden to the five or six others around it and the untamed hillside beyond them, and a cat had both sides of its bread buttered: the hiding places of the countryside, combined with none of the traditional accompanying worries about animal traps, and all the luxuries of cat suburbia.

As someone who had lived in plenty of towns, and plenty

of bits of country, such an odd mix of the two was new to me. By day, the birdlife created its own symphony, broken only by the sound of roadworks and a strange old man in a suit who stood on the other side of the lake and shouted, 'Fuckin' come on then! Let's be 'aving you!' at the ducks while they took his bread. By night, the ducks cackled loudly at the questionable cover versions of 'Ziggy Stardust' and 'Rebel Rebel' coming from the nearby pub. I was glad they were able to see the funny side of life, since with East Mendleham's thriving population of amateur teen rally drivers, the longevity of that life could never be counted as a given.

Seeing the bloodshed on the road, I was reminded of Brewer, but not without a new ambivalence, as I considered the destruction and heartbreak we were probably avoiding by not having him here with us. Fortunately, Shipley and Ralph, though sometimes liable to kid themselves other-wise, remained predominantly mice and vole men. The one time they did catch one of the lake's coots and bring it into the house, the bird was unharmed, and they immediately lost interest in it. If Dee and I were being paranoid, we could convince ourselves that they'd carried out the whole exercise purely for the comedic value of us chasing the bird around the living room like participants in a non-sexist, waterfowl-themed Benny Hill sketch. The humour of the situation was also not lost on Rory, the builder we were paying unreasonable sums of money to knock down several of our walls, who took a break from a cup of Tesco Value tea to watch the show.

After he had watched me perform five circuits of the rubble dividing our new kitchen from what used to be our bathroom, his face turned grave. 'Do you want me to finish if off for you?' he said, stepping forward with his pickaxe.

I assured him that I had the situation under control. While we both knew this wasn't remotely true, the fear of a potential beheading prompted me to redouble my efforts, and I grabbed a red bedspread off a drying rack and used it to steer the coot outside. I was relieved to see the bird sprint to freedom, but, standing at the back door, fabric in hand, I felt like the world's most inept matador.

Shipley and Ralph lost quite a bit of their hunter's instinct after that and entered a more supine phase, elucidating a confusing statistic I'd once read about cats spending 70 per cent of the day asleep and 30 per cent of it cleaning themselves. The same, however, could not be said for Rory.

Ever since he'd banged his head on our living room light shade and retaliated by ripping the top two buttons open on his shirt and shaking his fist at it, I'd been noticing how tightly wound he was. Hammering away at our surprisingly sturdy 1960s walls just didn't seem to be enough to satisfy his appetite for destruction. I hoped our new rooms would be finished before he finally burst his clothes and turned green, but the project was dragging on, so it seemed unlikely.

Living with builders is a bit like having to adopt an entirely new extended family for an extra-long Christmas, only to find that they piss on the floor, and say even more tactless things than your real extended family, there aren't any presents, and the turkey is actually not a turkey at all, but a quarter square of cold, leftover meat pie, welded to your new parquet floor. You try the best you can to exist in this artificial situation, ignoring the fact that the top floor of your house is now a rubble pit with a toilet in the middle, surrounded by orangey brown stains and copies of *The Sun*, but eventually matters get strained.

Over a course of several weeks, Rory and I had gradually

realised that we weren't quite the people we'd first mistaken one another for, in those early, forced, cheerful hours of the first couple of mornings when I'd made him and his ever-rotating cast of colleagues their first nineteen cups of tea. I had realised that when he said he 'didn't agree' with what George Bush was doing in Iraq, what he actually meant was he thought that the President should stop all this faffing around with ground troops and 'nuke the whole place'. He, in turn, had realised that his assumptions about me being 'pussy-whipped' by my wife's 'cat obsession' were not exactly true. Little clues must have given it away, like the time he looked out the window and saw me lying on the lawn, idly loading grass onto the back of a beatific Janet and feeding Shipley salt and vinegar crisps.

My relationship with Rory started to feel uncomfortably like a rerun of my pivotal second year at secondary school: the one where I won three playground fights and a place on the right wing of the under-14s football team, only to blow it all in the 'Write your Own Will' oral assignment in one unforgettable English lesson by announcing that, in the event of my death, I planned to bequeath my earthly pos-sessions to my pet cat, which I sometimes called 'The Ponce'.

As barbaric as their opinions can be, I find it useful to meet people like Rory from time to time, since they help to keep my animal-related soppiness in check. Obviously, it's a pain to lock up your bank statements while they're around and to grit your teeth while they make lewd comments at the female couriers who deliver packages to your house, but after a few days in their company you can't help but shine a new spotlight on the way you behave with your cats. These moments of reflection might not make a man stop asking his moggies about their day, or shelling out to have them chipped with electronic identity tags, but they help him to refrain from passing over to the Other Side: that dreaded one from which there is no return where, once settled in with his novelty leopard animal slippers under the coffee table, he will have no compunction about referring to himself as his pets' 'daddy' in formal company and dressing each of them in a £200 custom-made frilly waistcoat. I learned to keep my conversations with Shipley to a minimum around Rory, and when Dee and I had our discussion about giving Ralph female hormone therapy, we were sure to do so sotto voce.

The hormone therapy hadn't been our idea; it had been suggested by our new vet when we'd taken Ralph to see him to try to find a cure for his depression.

When you own four cats, the cost of veterinary care can mount up frighteningly quickly. If one of those cats has a very specific flea allergy and it happens to be vaccination time and you've got a claw-happy feral prowling the neighbourhood, you can be looking at £400 for a month's treatment before you know it. Unless you live in California, adding psychiatric care to this tally might seem somewhat unnecessary. On our most recent visit to the vet with Ralph, we hadn't exactly set out to get him psychoanalysed; we'd merely noticed that he hadn't been acting quite like himself recently and, observing that it was time for his latest flu jab, decided it couldn't hurt to make a discreet enquiry about his state of mind with a qualified professional.

'Cat ennui is actually quite common,' explained the effusive Yorkshireman in the white coat (did all vets have strong regional accents, or was it just mine?). 'Lots of different things can bring it on. A change of environment. A new cat on your cat's territory. A change of career.' He didn't actually say 'change of career' but for a moment I was convinced he was going to.

'The female hormones can sometimes help level the mood,' he continued, feeling beneath Ralph's armpits. 'Golly. You're a handsome devil, aren't you?'

'So in a way he'd be having his second sex change,' said Dee.

'How do you mean?' asked the vet.

'Long story,' we chimed.

As is perhaps to be expected from a male cat who'd been treated as a female for the first six months of his life, Ralph had always had a touch of the pretty boy about him. If he'd been a rock star, he would have been the airheaded kind who somehow manages to be simultaneously sexy and slightly fetid. Adulthood had turned him from merely beautiful to downright magnificent. To go with his bright white bib and the tabby flame on his forehead, an imperial ruff had burgeoned beneath and to the sides of his chin. It might be thought physically impossible for a cat covered head to toe in fur to be able to possess sideburns, but there was no more apt way to describe the grandiose flaps of fur at the side of his jowls, and Ralph liked nothing better to sport them with a droopy 'mousetache'.

However, as anyone who has been in the publicity team for a Warren Beatty press junket will probably attest, such magnificence requires its own special kind of sustenance. When The Bear permitted Dee or me to stroke his flanks and treated us to his special falsetto purr, or Shipley sang us 'The Chicken Song', or Janet headbutted us, the sense that we were partaking in an exchange of mutual respect may have been an illusion, but at least we had that illusion to cling to. When Ralph jumped onto our stomachs and began to knead us with his claws and dribble ecstatically, there *was* no illusion: we were there purely to remind him of his splendidness. This didn't actually feel like such a raw deal, since being in such close proximity to an animal so in touch with his own magnificence felt like something of a gift in itself.

You can see his shining, self-revelling Ralphness in our photos of him. Either these shots all just happened to be taken at times when he has just broken wind in an unusually satisfying manner, or that glint in his eye is the glint of an animal who knows that he is being worshipped and, as the descendant of Egyptian gods, such worship is his birthright.

When you see something as self-absorbed as that captured on film, it's difficult to resist the urge for sarcasm, and, as I stuck the photos in our albums, I would often add my own slightly derisory captions (e.g. 'I yam Ralph. Narcissism pleases me, but I have a girl's voice'). I knew, however, that his self-image was far from robust.

When people tell me that cats are independent animals unrequiring of attention, I can't help but immediately wonder if they've actually owned any. If they have, you can guarantee they're the kind of people who spend half their life moaning that their cats aren't as friendly as other people's. Cats might seem remote and self-sufficient, but it's all a great big front. Thousands of years of living with humans has taught them that by playing hard to get they can best shape us into what they need us to be, which is somewhere a cross between a cleaner, a chef, a masseur, a nurse and a supportive, ego-free friend to use as a sounding board for their greatest fears and darkest desires.

I'd always noticed how talking to my cats and stroking them made them calmer and more sociable. In Ralph's case, this applied tenfold. If we went a few days without being around to stroke or pet mitt him, or tell him he was a rock star, he could fade away so completely into the background that we half-expected to look at those beaming photos of him and see bits of them vanishing like the ones of Michael J. Fox's family in *Back to the Future*.

On the morning of our move itself, ten minutes before the removal men arrived, I'd had to make a last-minute dash to the vets, having found Ralph cowering in the kitchen, suffering from what can only be described as a very nasty rear-end blockage. The problem had cleared up after a few days ('Very unusual– it may just have been down to stress,' said the vet, a nice Swedish lady), but, for Ralph, the weeks that followed had been little more than an existentially futile, high-pitched journey from buddleia to laurel to hole in boiler room wall to pampas grass back to buddleia. I had no idea what was especially significant about the hole in the boiler room wall, but it must have had something going for it for him to spend an hour a day howling to be let in to stand and stare into it.

Ralph could skip and prance and trot when he wanted to, but he'd always had something a little doleful about his prowl. It was the gait of an animal seemingly forever slightly resentful that he couldn't walk on two legs. Now, though, as the summer stretched on, the mere act of moving from one bit of foliage to another at all looked like a genuine effort.

Picking up on his self-neglect, parasites would mark him out as an easy target. 'You look like you've slept in a hedge!' is hardly a wounding accusation to level at a cat, but, arriving indoors, he'd look like he'd slept in five, all at once. Even Janet, always the unbeaten master when it came to bringing shrubbery into the house via the rear of his body, was starting to look a little bit awestruck by the sheer variety of mixed media stuck to his kid step-brother's fur.

As I pulled leeches off Ralph's flanks and briars out of his feet and burned swollen, Satanic-pincered ticks off his neck, I was careful to be gentle, but it appeared to make little difference. I'd expected him to at least walk away from my grooming sessions with a bit of energetic indignance, blaming me for his pain, but his expression just said, 'Whatever, dude – it's all the same sticky outdoor crap to me.' Ten minutes later, he'd be back in a bush, killing us softly with his high-pitched song. If this had happened a couple of years previously, Dee and I would simply have said, 'Oh dear, Prudence is calling!' and gone back to our business. Now, all we could do was get him injected with girly drugs and hope for the best. But what if they took too much of a hold and made his sideburns disappear?

Our theories about the cause of his depression accumulated, both in number and hysteria. Was he belatedly missing his old pal Buttercup, or the other tabby from his litter: the one we'd been thinking about taking home, only to change our minds after seeing it fall asleep in its crud tray? Was he suffering from a rare summer form of seasonal affective disorder? Could his state of mind – and his new nervousness around garden tools – be the result of being chased out of a shed by one of our new neighbours? And, if so, why did he still persist in hiding in their gardens and whining?

Who knew what kind of experiences contributed to a cat's anxieties and phobias while it was out of your sight? DIY diagnosis was probably futile, and it was hard to tell if the female hormones had any effect, but I felt I could at least prescribe one home-grown remedy of my own – and one whose benefits would stretch far wider than Ralph's increasingly corpulent, forlorn form – and that was an intensive course of not moving or hacking into our home for at least the next couple of years.

It took almost six months for the builders to finish their work. The moment that they did so might have had its bittersweet aspects for the cats: they'd enjoyed licking those bits of leftover meat pie off the parquet floors, and living in a house entirely full of dirt, because we'd decided cleaning was futile, was not without its advantages. Janet, who had always timed his ample fluff deposits to perfection in the old days when we'd lived in places without two-inch layers of gunk all over their floors, visibly bristled as that indomitable metal foe of his, the vacuum cleaner, began to regain its self-respect and growl to life once again. The Bear, meanwhile, could not have been happy to see his favourite stair relieved of the seven different types of detritus stuck to it, including a pair of dried-up, hair-covered leaves which he probably had by now begun to regard like a couple of crinkly-skinned, wig-wearing relatives. He, more than any of the others, had weathered the latest round of upheaval stoically. But it was obvious to see how positively the departure of our temporary, pickaxe-wielding family affected each and every member of its permanent, four-legged counterpart.

The whole point of the building work had been to quickly reach the state of calmness that we'd been looking for ever since we first moved out of the big city. The problem was that in trying to achieve that, we'd trained ourselves to be anything but calm.

Maybe I did sometimes go outside and put grass on Janet's back or rescue a turtle, but, as soon as I had, I was instantly back inside having a discussion with Dee about steel joists or writing like the wind. Just like my cats saw bags of food miraculously appear as a result of me sitting at my computer and doing that odd thing with my hands, Rory and his cohorts must have thought the whole process was simple.

The way they saw it, they handed me an invoice, and I went downstairs to cover it by writing another article – in the same way that someone might write a shopping list. 'I wish I had an easy life,' they would say to us, after quizzing us about our jobs, supping their tea, not realising that the moment their banging stopped, Dee and I would rush to our respective posts – me in front of the brick dust-fogged computer screen downstairs, she upstairs packing antiques or contributing what she could to the building work in order to keep costs down – and work into the early hours, before being woken up by their drilling and banging.

It was a means to an end, we knew, but there comes a point when you realise that, whatever the joys that end you're working towards might promise, six months is a long time to be chewing dust and living in limbo amidst rubble. When we finally calmed down and gave ourselves a chance to breathe, it was Janet, Shipley, The Bear and Ralph who provided the most potent reminder of how bad we'd been at living in the moment. Was it really six months since we'd given out the Cat of the Month award? Since we'd bought The Bear a slightly unbecoming, emasculating fluorescent collar from Pets at Home? Since I'd seen a warm-furred Ralph sitting in the sun and sung him his own special version of Foreigner's 'Hot Blooded' ('Hot tabby! Check him and see! He's got a fever of a hundred and three . . .')? Where had we *been*?

We were back now, but it was another new year, a new spring – our fourth in Norfolk, already. We were here a bit later – and with a couple more bank loans – than planned, there was a rather ominous clanging in the pipes in our new bathroom and we were still finding bits of the builders' chewing gum stuck to the fridge, but on the plus side we seemed to have some contented cats, none of whom appeared to be crossing any roads, and our garden was once again coming to life in slightly unexpected ways. The turtle had taken the winter off, but by the first sunny day in April it was back on the jetty, and a couple of days later I looked out the window and saw a small brown hen pecking about on the lawn – a sighting which seemed relatively unspectacular, until you considered the problematic edifices it must have negotiated to get there and the fact that none of our near neighbours kept hens.

Though often very, very fond of chicken as a delicacy, the cats I've owned have always appeared uninterested in it in its animated form, making me wonder if, somewhere within the labyrinth of catiquette, there exists a special Poultry Code. Monty could have picked off any of my parents' bantam hens without breaking a sweat, but he made it clear such slaughter was beneath him. Daisy's desire for them, on the other hand, never really went further than a tendency to crouch low to the ground in their presence: an ostensibly predatory stance that became considerably less so once you realised her tendency to crouch low to the ground in the presence of pretty much everything from windfall apples to her own reflection.

Similarly, as Dee and I cornered this hen, the celebrated composer of 'The Chicken Song' seemed entirely preoccupied with some heavy-duty paw-cleaning. This proved to our advantage, since it meant that, by skilfully deploying the box that Dee's new computer had arrived in and a large plastic plant pot, we – well, I say 'we', Dee was responsible for the all-important dive – could capture it with a minimum of extraneous fuss. Nonetheless, it was a little bit of a workout. The perspiration on my forehead, combined with the hair that had accrued earlier on my somewhat adhesive black jumper while I'd been testing out a new pet mitt on

Ralph, must have created a rather odd impression when I rushed upstairs to answer the door to our new postlady. However, seemingly unperturbed by meeting a man who looked like he'd been interrupted in the middle of an illegal shearing experiment, she barely raised an eyebrow.

She seemed equally composed when I told her about the witless feathery animal currently locked in our bathroom.

'Chicken, you say? Hmm. I know a bloke who might be able to help you out. Fella lives a couple of doors up from me. If it's not one of his in the first place, I'm sure he'll be happy to take it. Just let me finish my round and I'll be back. I'm Phyllis, by the way.'

By this point in the day, the sun was shining brightly into our new open-plan dining room. It would be downright rude to hope for such a nice day in April usually, and Dee and I were savouring the prospect of a rare Saturday afternoon off. As we waited for Phyllis to return I was already rehearsing the phone conversations that would result from the day's events: my response to my mum the next time she asked me if I still liked my house ('Yeah, it's fine and the other day I gave a member of the Royal Mail a hen, which she drove away in her van, so I suppose it can't be that bad') and the rejoinders of our London friends ('Don't they have stamps in Norfolk?'). Sure enough, half an hour later, Phyllis returned, this time with a wooden carrier, replete with air holes.

After being assured that the package would be going to a loving home, we handed it over. By this time Shipley had joined us at the door. Fearing that he was having wistful thoughts of his Royal Mail-funded adventure in Trowse and poised to make a beeline for the van, I whisked him up into my arms and he offered Phyllis his Mohican to stroke.

'He's a nice boy, isn't he?' she said. 'He's not scared of

anybody, is he? Do you have another black one? A bit smaller than this one? My husband and I sometimes see him up near the road when we're coming back from the pub. He won't come near us but he looks right at us with these big adorable eyes. He's got ever such a cuddly round little face. We gave him a nickname, actually.'

'What was that?' I asked.

'Teddy,' she said.

IN MEMORIAM: A TRIBUTE TO A FEW
OF THE OTHERS WE HAVE LOST

1. Fat Rat (May 2002)

The too-remote, too-gloomy starter cottage is on the market. Dee and I have been watching *House Doctor* religiously for what feels like the last seventeen years, without stopping. Colour schemes have become neutral. Surfaces have been Flash-wiped to within an inch of their lives. Coffee has been brewed. That large, suspiciously brown leaf has been picked off Janet's formidable fluffy posterior at the last minute. Mr Newman has arrived. 'It's like the Tardis in here,' he says. 'Nice garden, too.' But, oh, what's that? It's the world's biggest rat, leaping out out of the antique po cabinet, and running across the room squeaking comically! That smooth operator from *Selling Houses* on Channel 4 never had this trouble.

2. Twangy Stoat (April 2003)

The length of a human intestine is approximately twenty-two feet. The length of a stoat's intestine, meanwhile, is not notably shorter. I know this. Why? Because I have seen one stretched out to its full length across my lawn.

3. Giant Green Leechslug (August 2004)

Easily the most large and disgusting of the things Ralph has had feeding off him. Gave Dee a month's worth of nightmares after she cut it off him: 'Every time I dream of it, I dream that I'm cutting part of his body.'

4. Lower Portion Double-Decker Mouse (November 2004)

'I've caught it!' said Dee, holding the mini muesli box aloft in triumph, containing Shipley's victim. 'And it seems to have all its legs intact!' she continued, making her way to the garden to set it free. 'Oh no!' she shouted ten seconds later, slightly less triumphantly, after realising she had set it free directly onto the back of one of its deceased contemporaries. 'Do you think they mind about that kind of thing?'

5. Forlorn Blobby Mass (March 2005)

Just because your identity was nebulous, do not think that you do not merit the term 'plucky'. You did not go to the wheelie bin without a fight, little man/creature/thing/viscous gloop – you were an absolute bugger to get off the entrance hall floor, and you will be remembered.

Crouching Puma, Hidden Bear

While we both agree on the basic circumstances, the finer details of what caused us to almost end up owning seven cats remains a point of contention. Dee maintains that everything got out of control because I went to the Celia Hammond Animal Trust (CHAT) and came home feeling my moral obligation to house a quarter of the UK's unwanted felines more acutely than ever. I admit she has a valid point, but I remember that everything really started with a rough estimate about the weight of a beagle.

Ever since Dee and I had been together, we'd periodically had conversations about owning dogs. Actually, ever since we'd been together, we'd periodically had conversations about owning goats, pigs, capybaras, donkeys, llamas, sheep, bonobo chimpanzees, tiger cubs, pandas, giant rabbits, chipmunks and wallabies as well, but the ones about dogs had more of an intent, summit-like quality about them and had come up increasingly frequently, particularly since we'd left Staithe Cottage and began to miss our time with Nouster.

It would all invariably start when the cats were being

particularly arsey with us, or I began to fantasise about having an animal that would sit obediently at my feet and look up adoringly at me while I worked. We'd usually discuss the matter and come to the conclusion that we were quite content owning animals that can take care of their own excretory needs and that dogs are both too easy to live with and too hard to live with in all the wrong ways. But in early 2005, a decline in Dee's health meant we considered the canine question at further length than usual.

All her life, Dee had suffered from migraines. In years gone by, these would occur every month or two. Two or three hours in a darkened room and she'd be back on form. But more recently, particularly after her Yosemite Sam-like run of head injuries, the migraines had increased severely in both frequency and strength. One second, she'd be typing or reading or speaking to someone on the phone; the next, she'd look down at her fingers and be unable to see them. She began to forget basic words, stutter and use phrases that seemed to come from completely different sentences. We were both extremely frightened. An MRI scan and tests at the neurologist's failed to provide a definitive answer to what was wrong, and only led to more tests. Having begun a new job at an arts centre ten miles from our house, she was forced to quit. Tablets provided by her GP only made her sleepy and even more confused. We started to wonder just what kind of long-term toll all these knocks and jolts had taken.

Dee's inspirational step-grandma, Chrissie, suffered a stroke at the age of seventeen, and attributed her full recovery at least partly to surrounding herself with animals. With this in mind, we thought the fresh air and unconditional cuddles that went hand-in-hand with dog ownership could only help Dee's cause.

But, as so often before, when it came right down to it, we couldn't quite see ourselves as dog owners. Yes, we liked saying 'Hello!' in overexaggerated posh voices to dogs on the street. But did we want a ball of hyperactive, wagging idiocy getting under our feet on a daily basis? Maybe not.

Ultimately, we liked to feel we had to work for affection from our animals, even when one of us was ill. We also concluded that a beagle, Dee's favourite type of dog, might be the last straw as far as The Bear was concerned. We'd seen his look of resentful disbelief when he'd been reunited with Janet upon first moving to Norfolk, then seen that look grow as he'd met the nascent Brewer, Shipley and Ralph, and come to terms with the scandalous realisation that, from now on, he would be cohabiting with six lesser intellectual beings, rather than just three. Who knows what would have happened if we introduced the Real Enemy – the ultimate dumbo foe – into the house? It could have pushed him over the edge . . . or at least into the crawl space beneath the Upside Down House, where he would probably stay indefinitely, refusing to groom himself, making sculptures out of mouse corpses and planning how exactly, when the right moment came, he would dispose of the six frivolous individuals above him.

To be fair on myself, by the time I arrived at the Canning Town branch of CHAT, I was probably not in one of my more robust mental states. As well as fretting about Dee's head, I'd been woken up early by the sound of Shipley destroying a box of tissues and waylaid by a damp-smelling man outside Canning Town tube station who wouldn't let me past until he'd imparted some hugely vital details to me about a revolution involving stick insects. I'd been dispatched to meet Celia Hammond by one of my newspaper editors, who wanted me to interview her about her cat

rescue work and her past as a high profile 1960s super-
model.

A friend who volunteered at another branch of CHAT
had told me that, while living with the rock star Jeff Beck
during the seventies, Hammond would sneak rescue animals into Beck's castle, until finally the place was overrun
with more than 100 cats and dogs. Nowadays her life was
completely dictated by cats in a way that even I could barely
imagine. By day, she would take dozens of them in out of the
cold, neuter them, feed them. By night, she would go on
midnight raids, rescuing strays from the site where the 2012
London Olympic Village was being constructed.

When I asked what time I should stop by the Canning
Town branch, one of her colleagues told me, 'Oh, just turn
up – Celia lives here.' It was only when I arrived that I
realised she was not using a figure of speech: Celia really *did*
live in this unprepossessing building on Canning Town
High Street, grabbing at most a couple of hours' sleep per
night on a couch in a cramped kitchen at the back of the
building strewn with cardboard boxes, Whiskas tins and
perma-stained coffee mugs.

Having led me into this room and offered me a seat on an
old towel, Celia told me somewhat dismissively about her
past as a friend to Mick Jagger and Twiggy. She then handed
me a tiny yelping black and white kitten and a container of
milk, while she took a phone call from a woman who had
thrown her cat out onto the street 'because it had fleas' and
then found neighbourhood children trying to kill it with
sticks. Today, Celia told me, was a 'quiet day', which I soon
came to understand to mean that the phone only rang with
another report of feline woe once every minute, instead of
once every twenty seconds.

By the time Celia had shown me into the main area where

the recent influx of vagabonds and orphans were kept, I knew I was in trouble. The tiny yelping kitten had reminded me of Brewer and I'd had to get a vice-like grip on myself to leave it behind, but as soon as the roly-poly ginger in the third cage along and I set eyes on one another, there was an unmistakable chemistry in the air. 'How many cats precisely could one fit with them on the Liverpool Street to Norwich train, without causing upset to one's fellow travellers?' I wondered. For not the first time that day, I decided it was a good thing I had not brought the car with me.

Before I'd been to CHAT, I'd often seen signs for cat rescue centres whilst out driving and had a barely controllable urge to hit the indicator. But I had always talked myself out of it, knowing that I would only come away with a new mouth to feed or a fresh wave of impotent rage at an unfeeling universe. Somehow, calling on some unsuspected reserve of self-discipline, I managed to walk out of Celia's place empty-handed, but it wasn't long before the old guilt kicked in. How could I go blithely about my day-to-day existence knowing there were cats out there being hit with sticks, cats getting covered in glue and paint, cats – really surprisingly plush-looking cats, who would probably happily sit on your knee for up to three hours without budging – languishing in cages, unwanted? Yes, Dee and I were already taking care of a gaggle of feline misshapes, and, yes, we were fighting a losing battle against the mud stains on our stairs, but wasn't it my duty as a Cat Man to make my use of the meagre cup I'd been handed to help bail out the sinking ship? After all, if you totted up the strays at Canning Town, the Lewisham branch of CHAT and the home in the Sussex countryside that she almost never visited, Celia had roughly 600 more cats than me, and did you hear her complaining about mud on *her* stairs?

'So, sod it, let's get another,' said Dee, when I told her about my experience at CHAT. 'I mean, bloody hell, we were almost going to get a medium-sized dog. That would have been loads more work than another cat.'

'It would probably weigh as much as two of them, for a start,' I added.

'Oh, at least! And besides, I've had enough of living with five blokes. It's time I had some female company around here.'

Having been a firsthand witness to much of the long, fraught story of Dee's search for an extra female around the house, I was only too keen to help her find a girl moggy without male genitalia. Our visit to the Kentford RSPCA in Suffolk the following day yielded an immediate candidate.

Ginny, who in more refined feline circles would have been probably referred to as a 'Blue', couldn't have made her motives more obvious if she'd whispered 'Get me out of here – I'll make it worth your while!' into our ears. She was clearly a creature with an enormous capacity for love, but, after we'd spent two minutes taking turns letting her cling to us, our long-sleeved T-shirts were starting to resemble mohair sweaters.

There was something else that was unusual about Ginny, a familiar look about her that I couldn't quite place. Dee was the one to put her finger on it.

'She looks like your mum,' she said.

I'd never met an animal that resembled one of my parents before and I discovered I had mixed feelings about it. I suppose if you bear in mind the popular theory that most dogs look like their owners, then it wouldn't have been that unusual to have a cat that reminded me of one of the people whose genes I share. But I couldn't quite squish visions of

Ginny interfering with decisions about household decorating, reminding me to drive carefully and telling Dee that I'd 'always been boisterous'.

Keeping our options open, we moved on to the next run.

'Here are Ethel and Austin,' said Gillian, the jolly welly-wearing lady from the RSPCA. 'They're brother and sister, but they need to be separated, we think, because Ethel needs to come out of Austin's shadow.'

As Austin (grey, stunted) began to climb up my head and inspect my hair for hidden rodents, I looked across at Dee, who was having a far less rough-and-tumble encounter with Ethel (grey, boss-eyed, even more stunted). I only had to take in the sensually arching back and gently flexing claws (Ethel's, not Dee's) and the faraway look in the eyes (Dee's and Ethel's) to know how this would end.

'So, she's definitely female?' I asked Gillian. 'You're absolutely sure?'

'Oh yes, absolutely no doubt about it.'

We stepped towards the next three runs, saying hello to Popsy (white and black), Shuttlecock (jet black) and two brothers, Bourneville and Cadbury (black and browny-black), but being sure to move quickly, for fear of racking up yet more emotional attachments. In doing so, we knew that we were fundamentally unscrupulous people. 'The Black Cat', Edgar Allan Poe's famous story of a feline provoking madness and murder and its vengeance, was over a century and a half old, but it still said a lot about the raw deal given to society's darker common-or-garden feline. Black cats might have been welcomed into households across the world, but their oppressed past as the victims of slaughter and superstition still tainted them. As Celia Hammond had told me, 'It's rare that people come here looking for a black one.'

I was sure that it was pure chance that had led to Ginny, Austin and Ethel being given pole position in the runs ahead of their witchy compatriots. I'm equally sure, however, that, by making a fuss over the more exciting colours and overlooking the more everyday hues in the runs beyond them, we were doing just what every other cat hunter at Kentford that week had done before us.

But what else could be expected of us? I could see that there was no going back for Dee and Ethel now. I suppose I could have told Shuttlecock, Bourneville and Cadbury that some of my best cat friends were black, and cited the examples of Janet, Shipley and The Bear waiting for us at home, but I doubt that would have cut the mustard with them.

The final bit of cat housing on the row appeared to be empty.

'This is Raffles,' said Gillian. 'He's sleeping at the moment.'

Somewhere in the dark at the back of the run – the part that formed a sort of cat treehouse, without a tree – I saw a big black shape stir. I peered in, hopefully, but had a strange instinct not to get too close. A second later, an enormous muzzle – the kind of muzzle that begged to to be celebrated, the kind of muzzle that more primitive civilisations would have mounted in memoriam – poked its way out of the entrance hole, and lolled on the wood.

'Brrroaaaaaghwww,' it said, insouciantly.

I took a step back, almost falling onto the gravel path behind me.

'He's a big boy, isn't he?' said Gillian.

In truth, the answer was no: Raffles wasn't big. 'Big' was what Ralph, Janet and Shipley were. Visitors to our house would often comment on their size and jokingly ask if we fed them out of buckets. But if I had ever taken one of them out for a walk into East Mendleham town centre on a lead, the only stares I would have got would probably have been for being weird enough to take a cat out shopping with me. If I took this beast out, however, passers-by would bow down before me in deference. 'Look! It's that bloke with the puma,' the local yobs would say, tipping their baseball caps as I went by. Pretty soon, I'd be one of the town's most notorious characters, right up there with that bloke who shouted 'Fuckin' come on then! Let's be 'avin you!' to the birds and the old man who sometimes busked outside the Co-op and got his Border collies to howl in time with his ukulele.

Coming out of my reverie, I stepped gingerly into the run and offered a tentative couple of arms in Raffles's direction. Languidly, he stepped into them, then began working on my shoulder with his paws, which would have been extremely pleasant, if I hadn't come out in a rush and left my chainmail suit hanging on the chair next to my wardrobe.

'Oh dear,' said Dee to Gillian. 'I think this could be the start of a beautiful friendship.'

If we had been buying a car, this was the point where Dee and I would have moved away into a quiet corner and begun to debate the merits of the two models we had been perusing, and whether the salesman was being straight with us. I would have argued for the added boot size and masculine appearance of the Ford Cougar, Dee would have made a case for the cuter and more economical Nissan Figaro, and we would have met somewhere in the middle or, more likely, decided to put off our purchase until another day, then forgotten about it altogether.

The problem was that getting a new cat was so much easier than that. Gillian had little to gain from lying about how old Ethel (four months) and Raffles (ten years) were and the £40 donation fee wasn't going to be an issue. Dee and I made a brief pretence of huddling together for a hushed discussion, but, really, what more was there to consider? I had found a cat I loved. Dee had found a cat she loved.

An hour later, we arrived home with one very overstuffed cat basket. Dee had recently read a book by a cat behaviour expert which suggested that the introduction of new cats into a household should be staggered, and since Ethel was due to be neutered at the RSPCA in two days' time, we decided to wait a few days to collect her, giving Raffles a chance to mingle with The Bear, Janet, Ralph and Shipley.

I've seen enough cats getting used to new homes now to be able to tick off the four inevitable stages of settling in: the random sniffing; that bit where they start checking all the walls, as if believing there's a safe or hidden entrance behind them; the sheepish dart under the bed. The creeping emergence three hours later, as bowel functions and appetite triumph over nerves. Raffles, however, was an anomaly. Never, even after a routine trip to the vets, had I seen one of my pets stroll quite so confidently out of his basket. Within a minute, he was sitting proudly on the arm of the sofa, licking a paw and nonchalantly surveying his territory. If there had been a thought bubble above his head, it would probably have said, 'Don't get me wrong. I like this in the suede, but personally my taste runs more to leather.'

'Raffles!' I said, in my deepest voice, sensing he was not the kind of cat to be treated with kid gloves. 'Come here.'

I patted my knee, and he made his way over to me in a fashion that reminded me of the overfed boss from a mafia film I'd just seen. When I called cats that I owned and they came to me this instantaneously, it was invariably either because I was holding a meat-based snack or they had muddy paws and required a surface upon which to blot them off, but here there seemed to be no ulterior motive.

Again, the kneading started. I was glad that the surface protecting me was corduroy this time, but I was a bit worried about its proximity to some of the more tender parts of my anatomy. I was used to this sort of thing from Ralph – the main difference being a) that Ralph's claws had little in common with Freddie Kruger's, and b) the accompanying noise. What was coming from Raffles's mighty muzzle probably passed for a purr of fair-to-middling strength, but only in a magical meaty land where Iams grew on trees and cats were as big as buses.

Aided by the contrast provided by my other cats, I now began to get a further sense of Raffles's enormity. Shipley was the first to come and see what all the fuss was about. The expression on his face was the most flabbergastedly human of a life that had already contained many astonishingly person-like moments. If I'd ever thought cats were too cool to do double-takes, I now realised I was wrong. For Shipley, who had always been possessive towards me, what he saw before him perhaps constituted the ultimate insult: not just a bigger cat at large in his domain, working his claws steadily in the direction of his owner's groin, but a bigger cat that looked quite a bit like him, only with an extra third of muscle and heft.

Raffles's movement was a decisive one that managed to combine speed with a look of slow-motion laziness. In a panicked flick and a nervous flurry, Shipley was out the cat-flap and cowering on the patio.

Raffles returned to my feet, and looked up at me. His sleepy eyes said, "T'was nothing, fine sir, but any rewards gratefully accepted nonetheless.'

'I'm sure things will calm down soon,' said Dee, after

she'd arrived in the room to find out what the commotion was.

She was right: by 11 p.m. that night, things had calmed down considerably. This was mainly because our house now only contained one cat. When we had gone to bed, there had been none of the usual coaxing and bribing that it took to get our pets on the bed on the occasions we really wanted them there, none of the usual celebrity tantrums or walk-outs when we adjusted the duvet an inch or two beneath them. Raffles simply strolled in casually behind us, then made his way onto the bed, where he lay, vibrating deeply, looking up at us with unbridled love.

'Where the hell is everyone?' asked Dee.

Getting up for a glass of water, I took a peek outside onto the patio. Here I found four wide-eyed animals who had put aside their squabbles and vendettas, some of which stretched back years, to become united in fear and incomprehension.

There have been countless times when I have wished I could talk to my cats and explain the ins and outs of a difficult situation, but this was not one of them. If I had been able to speak meowese, what could I possibly have said? 'That woman you think of erroneously as your mother had not been feeling well, so we decided that, because none of you were being particularly cuddly, we would get another cat who might be more cuddly. Yes, I know his head is twice as big as a 3-year-old child's, but try to ignore the intimidation factor and look on the bright side. If you're lucky and don't get in his face too much he might even occasionally let you eat'?

Or maybe: 'I am perfectly aware we already have three black cats, and you're all very nice, and some would say that really is enough but it's true: we got one more. Think of it as a homage. And please don't think it's because we don't love you, because we do. Oh yes: one other thing. Did I tell you there's another one arriving in seven days' time? But she's grey and very small, so you'll probably be able to take out your frustration by pushing her around'?

Three days later, I did something that I thought I'd never do, and that I hope I will never do again, as long as I live: I returned a cat. There are the usual bonding and territory marking problems you get when adding to your feline family, and then there is outright tyranny, and Dee and I would not have been able to live easily with the knowledge that our out-of-control cat love – and, more specifically, my preposterous macho cat fantasy – had led us to alienate our gang of long-serving four-legged friends.

I gave Raffles a Raffles-size hug when I arrived back at the RSPCA with him, knowing that, two weeks later, I'd still have the chest scars to prove it. He didn't look upset. He was a big man, and he could take rejection. But the bewilderment would surely kick in sooner or later, like that of a wrongly convicted prisoner who had been rescued from Alcatraz and been given his own Bel Air mansion with butler service, only to be hurled back into the clink, without explanation, as soon as he had made himself at home. He didn't even get the privilege of being transferred to one of the more prominent runs. It was back to his old spot in the relegation zone – a place reserved for old cats and black cats, but primarily a place reserved for old black cats. I couldn't shake my conviction that, in his big, stolid, philosophical way, he would spend the days that followed resting his comedy-sized chin on the edge of his treeless treehouse, wondering what he had done wrong. Leaving Kentford, close to tears, I made Gillian promise that she would let us know as soon as he had been rehomed.

Those three days had been difficult ones for all of us. Shipley hadn't let his Mohican down past half mast the whole time, and Janet stuck his tongue out in a manner suggestive of utter incomprehension that there could be a black cat in the house more hulking than he was.

Ever since Phyllis had told us about 'Teddy' hanging about near the road, we'd been telling ourselves that she was talking about another, less well-behaved bearish black cat, but just before I'd finally given up trying to persuade everyone to come back into the house on Raffles's first night, I'd seen a small black bottom make a telltale journey over the fence. The only sighting of The Bear in the sixty hours that followed was a flash of two big furious green eyes beneath the pampas grass. Most sad of all, perhaps, was the case of Ralph, who seemed to have fully shaken off last year's summer affective disorder and had been enjoying the rainy late winter and spring. In a particularly chirpy mood the day after Raffles's arrival, he somehow contrived to forget all about his new enemy's presence in the house, and burst happily into the bedroom only to be cornered by a huge black mass of claws and dribble. In the past, we'd often called Ralph himself by the nickname Raffles. Obviously he didn't know that he'd had his name stolen along with his territory – come to think of it, he probably didn't even know he was called Ralph either – but it somehow seemed to highlight the aching ignominy all the more.

If Raffles had been a bad cat – a cat who behaved aggressively towards us, as well as towards his own kind, a decision could have been made much more easily. As it was, however, everyone was helpless. Ralph, Shipley, The Bear and Janet couldn't help the fact that they suddenly had as much

chance of getting a quiet sleep in our living room as they
had of surviving in the jungles of Vietnam. Raffles couldn't
help the fact that he liked us so much that he wanted us
completely to himself. And, as fond as we were of him, we
couldn't help the fact that such fondness could not be put
above the more binding kind that has been developed with
our pets over many years.

In just one way, perhaps, we could have made the situation very slightly easier.

In the flurry of Raffles's arrival, Dee and I hadn't had
a chance to check our answerphone. It wasn't until the
following morning that we'd found the message from
Dorothy, the woman at Suffenham Parva Cat Rehoming
Centre, a few miles south of East Mendleham. This was
in response to the enquiry Dee had made with them about
their current residents before our trip to the RSPCA. It
explained that they had a 'beautiful ginger boy' who was a
little bit timid, but extremely keen on the company of other
cats, and looking for a good home.

At such a juncture, most sensible people might have surveyed the four animals quivering outside their back door
and the zoo-worthy exhibit languidly stretching its back
legs in their living room and declared that enough was
enough. But, Dee and me being Dee and me, we reached
straight for the car keys.

'It can't hurt to go and have a look at him, can it?' we
asked. 'Haven't we always said that ginger cats have sunny
personalities?' we asked. We did not ask, 'What if Raffles
tears off his head and uses it as a pillow?'

Dorothy, from whose rambling Elizabethan house the
Suffenham Parva Cat Rehoming Centre operated, had mentioned on the phone that Beautiful Ginger Boy had been
found living in a derelict farmhouse with more than a dozen

of his brothers and sisters. Before she rescued him, it had been the RSPCA's intention to put him to sleep.

'Of course,' she thought to add, as she met us at the end of her drive, 'you do have to understand that he is feral.' I could see why she might not have wanted to mention the 'f' word until she'd got us captive. I'm sure I wasn't in the minority of cat owners in viewing ferals in the same way as a protective parent might view a gang of hoodlums who regularly stole his or her offspring's packed lunch. These were the feline outlaws who shunned my outstretched hand, left their scent on my pot plants and could almost certainly be held responsible for the lamentable state of The Bear's right ear. It wasn't that I didn't want to help them learn to love and be loved, more that I'd long ago come to the understanding that trying to do so would be as futile as attempting to teach a crab algebra.

'Of course,' said Dorothy, 'the thing about ferals that a lot of people don't know is that most of them actually get on very well with other cats. They're actually very easygoing. I've got eight of my own. I'm telling you, once you go feral, you don't go back.'

Intrigued as I was to hear this, I can't say that my first glance inside the cage in her garage went further towards shattering my preconceptions. The cat lurking there was undoubtedly ginger, and the acrid waft of testosterone that surrounded him pretty much confirmed he was a boy, but easygoing? And beautiful? Beauty was a hard thing to get a handle on, when an animal was this obviously petrified and underweight. Dorothy's decision to hold his scruff and present him to us on his hind legs, so as to highlight his bulging eyes and protruding tongue, did little to detract from the aura of wildness.

If Dee and I spent longer with Beautiful Ginger Boy than

we had done when choosing our other cats, it was perhaps because he didn't seem that much like a cat at all. Certainly, he had the tail and the cold pink nose and the pointy ears and some of the whiskers ('the others got chopped off in the trap when the RSPCA caught him,' said Dorothy) but his pelt had the rough, dry feel more readily associated with an animal you'd find in a warren than a living room.

As we stroked and encouraged, that tongue refused to retract. After about ten minutes, though, something happened. You wouldn't have quite called it a purr; it was more like a tiny, just-tangible softening of Beautiful Ginger Boy's breathing. I'd like to say it was the clincher, but in truth Dorothy had had us at hello. All we needed now was a name. On the way to the Rehoming Centre, we'd been having a discussion about brilliantly unlikely cat monikers. Rejecting my perverse suggestions of Gary and Wayne on obvious grounds of taste, Dee had said she had always wanted to have a cat called Pablo, so we decided to go for that.

If I had any concerns about introducing a feral cat to a giant feline extraterrestrial, they were put to bed within about five minutes of getting home. I'd expected more of the same quivering terror we'd seen from Pablo at Suffenham Parva, but within a moment of seeing Raffles stalk across the bedroom, he suddenly became lit from inside, emitted an elated, stuttering squeak, and scuttled up alongside him. It was one of the most effusive cat hellos I'd ever witnessed, and Raffles swatted it away as a dauntless explorer might swat away a tiny gnat in the periphery of his vision. He had bigger fish to fry – 'fry' in this case meaning 'stare at in an intimidating, room-owning fashion' and fish meaning 'cats' (and, in all probability, 'fish').

Undaunted, upon being let out of the bedroom to roam

the following day, Pablo proceeded to greet Janet, Ralph, Shipley and The Bear the same way, eliciting varying degrees of indifference.

We had been lucky. Who could have said what kind of disquiet might have ensued if Pablo had conformed more squarely to the feral stereotype of the flighty troublecauser? Or maybe Dorothy was right, and all ferals were this gregarious? Whatever the case, Pablo's status as a born cat's cat only highlighted Raffles's incompatibility and confirmed that we would be doing the right thing by taking him out of the equation.

Further confirmation arrived when we returned from our next bittersweet trip to Kentford with Ethel – now renamed Bootsy – who proved much more receptive to Pablo's advances than her four new housemates. But on the way home, fully conscious that we had swapped an ageing, demanding outsider cat for a young, easygoing, easy-on-the-eye cat, my conscience played havoc with me. It was a bigger version of that feeling I'd had on the way back home with Monty after the death of Tabs, but this time I knew that the sight of Pablo and Bootsy running up the curtains – that is, if they had the time for running up the curtains, between cuddling each other – wasn't going to be such an instant cure.

East Mendleham is a place of countless retail contradictions: a town bafflingly equipped with no less than four key-cutting outlets, but only one shop selling paint; a place where a person might search in vain for hours in an attempt to get a half-decent sandwich or apple, but find three different shops specializing in bags of dried fruit. Just one of its many oddly conceived stores was the place where I tended to buy my cats' food during 2005, which, in addition to doing a good line in optimised biscuity nutrition and meaty chunks, also sold rather a lot of camera equipment.

Who knows? Perhaps the owner of Mattock Pet and Camera was convinced that there was an untapped market in people who liked to take snaps of their cats as they chowed down on Applaws' chicken and cheese range, or maybe he just really, really liked cats, dogs and cameras? It was perhaps a testament to the mixed-up nature of the shop that the biggest picture of a cat – well, a puma, to be precise – was on a poster advertising a zoom lens.

With the wretch-like Pablo tucking into every meal like it was his last, I had cause to stare upon this puma frequently in the weeks following Raffles's departure, and its resemblance to my rejected pet was uncanny.

'Oh,' it would say to me, gazing judgementally down from above the counter, 'here again buying food for your other cats, are you? That's *nice*. I bet they're pretty too, aren't they. It's good to be *kind* to cats and to feed them and *home* them. So awful when they end up spending their last good years stuck out in the cold with nobody to take care of them. But don't you worry about me. I'll just soldier on, until pneumonia or senility kicks in and then, one day, not long after that, my kind dies out altogether, and there are only interestingly coloured, young, good-looking cats around, and you'll be able to sleep easy in your nice, warm, comfy bed. Which reminds me, do you still have that old fluffy towel at the bottom of it?'

The cat wants what the cat wants: I only had to look at the six layabouts sprawled decadently on forbidden surfaces all over my house to realise that. But how could I hold such id-led behaviour against them, when I was no better?

Sure, I could come up with a practical 'reason' to explain

why I'd got each of my six existing cats. I could tell myself that Janet and The Bear were inherited, and Shipley and Ralph had been procured to celebrate our new life together, and Bootsy was the girl cat that Dee had always wanted and Pablo was my own personal first genuine 'project' cat. I could look at Bootsy and see a cat that was cuddly, attentive, soothing: a cat that was almost too perfect to be true for Dee, in her convalescing state. I could look at Pablo and see a cat who, though still scratchy and bare of fur and nervous of disposition, seemed to somehow know he'd faced a near-death experience and be genuinely grateful for his new home comforts. But I'd be kidding myself if this was all about benevolence, and there was no greed involved. The Raffles debacle had given me a glimpse of the dark-side, shown me just how easily it could be for someone to love cats too much for the good of the cats in their path.

I asked around among our friends to find out if anyone would be interested in Raffles, but got no takers. His sure-footed manner would probably have appealed to my dad, but I didn't want to be responsible for giving The Slink a heart attack. Several times, I picked up the phone to call Gillian at the RSPCA to find out how he was, but I knew that if I'd spoken to her about Raffles, my picture of him alone in his run would have been that much clearer, and that would have made me want to go to see him.

Such a visit would only have ended up with me coming home with him to give it one more try, quite probably with three of his prisonmates, or bedding down for the night in empathy in the cage next to him.

It's hard to say what would have happened if Gillian hadn't called when she did to tell us that Raffles had been rehomed with 'a nice man in his fifties who lived on his own'. By then it had been almost four weeks since I'd first met him, but I'd barely gone an hour without thinking about him. Who knows, perhaps I would have kept pressing down on the lid of that old internal suitcase housing my cat conscience until it finally burst open more violently than ever before, causing me to give up my job, sell all my worldly possessions, Celia Hammond-style, and start my own cattery, with Raffles as the in-house ambassador.

As it was, the fantasy drifted away, and things settled back down into a kind of normality – or at least as close to normality as one can achieve, when they're on twenty-four-hour call for six separate sets of whiskers. Dee's health improved, Pablo's tongue stayed out, Shipley's Mohican subsided, and Dee and I started to come to the realisation that, while we may have narrowly avoided stepping over one line, we had nevertheless stepped over another: namely, the one that made us no longer 'people who own a lot of cats' and suddenly 'The People Who Own All the Cats'. There were mouths to feed, testicles to get removed, stairs to clean, a never-more-competitive Cat of the Month award to invigilate. But every so often, I'd take a moment to think about where Raffles might be now.

His new owner would be a big man, I imagined, who favoured heavily insulated clothing and lived a simple, out-doors-orientated life. I saw him as the kind of rugged, dependable, middle-aged bachelor one scarcely sees outside books by Annie Proulx and Jane Smiley: an architect, or a boat builder, perhaps. Whilst hesitantly petting a Dobermann at Kentford, he would have looked across idly at the adjacent cat kennels, and had his interest piqued by a flash of dark muscle.

Side by side ever since, he and Raffles would now spend comfortable, stoic evenings together strolling across heathland and reclining beside an open fire in his self-built A-frame. At the end of the night, before going to bed, he would put another log on the fire for Raffles, after which my former cat would rest his legendary muzzle on the hardwood floor and begin to purr like a big soft machine. Never one to spend an overt amount of time living in the past or future, he'd give little thought to tomorrow's leftover bacon breakfast, or the cold nights he'd spent in his treeless treehouse at the RSPCA, wondering if there was anyone out there in the universe for him. But I hoped that, before he closed his eyes, he'd take just a second to remember the life that nearly was, with that other bloke – the one who wasn't quite as good at DIY and didn't own quite as many plaid shirts – and his wife, both of whom would have liked to have given him the life he needed but couldn't. And I hoped that, as he did, he'd feel no bitterness, only a sense of peace, and destiny, and what could never be, and of what it feels like to be finally, properly Home.

I WOULD DO ANYTHING FOR CATS (BUT I WOULDN'T DO THAT): NINE OF THE MANY THINGS I WOULD NEVER EVER DO IN THE NAME OF MOGGY LOVE

1. Get the names of my favourite two cats tattooed inside a heart on my back, with the words 'For Ever' inscribed beneath it in gothic lettering.

2. Name a star in honour of one or more of my cats.

3. Encourage one of my cats to eat by taking a mouthful of its food, then rubbing my stomach and saying 'Yum yum yum.'

4. Check my cats' horoscopes.

5. Sit my cats down in a circle and read them said horoscopes.

6. Purchase a cat pushchair.

7. Abandon essential household furniture in order to make way for elaborate oversized scratching posts or imported 'cat condos' (e.g. the Naughty Paws Bungalow: RRP $475).

8. Refer to myself unironically as my cats' 'daddy' (well, not in public, anyway).

9. Purchase a dressing gown with the name of a cat food manufacturer embroidered on it or save up 'bonus points' then send off for said garment free of charge.

Golfing for Cats

When I was little, I was told that on the continent people didn't just drive on the other side of the road, they also stroked cats backwards. I forget the source of this information now. Perhaps it was a children's book. Alternatively, it could have been a jocular elderly relative or friend of my parents. Whatever the case, I have since found it to be untrue. The place that people actually stroke cats backwards is Birmingham.

'Come on!' said Joyce, a lady in her late fifties with a strong Yorkshire accent and a fleece, to Barbara, another lady in her late fifties with an even stronger Yorkshire accent and a fleece. 'Really fluff it up. Do it. You know he likes it. Oh yes! That's right. That's right.'

Joyce and Barbara were the owners of one of the contestants at the Supreme Cat Show, the feline answer to Crufts held at the Birmingham NEC, and I'd been watching them, mesmerised, for around ten minutes. I'm not sure why, out of all the fancy and exotic looking cats in the auditorium, I'd chosen to stop and look at Dukey, their Selkirk rex. Perhaps it was because he was the first cat I'd ever seen up close that

looked like a giant furry caterpillar. Now Joyce had started
going at him with the brush, he was looking even more like
a furry caterpillar, but he didn't seem to mind.

'So is it okay to stroke and brush him like that?' I said,
watching as Joyce fiercely brushed his fur back against the
grain, thinking: if I did this to The Bear, he'd piss in my
kitchen blender.

'Oh yes,' she said. 'You have to stroke them like this. It's
the way they're bred. To like it.'

'So why do you call him Dukey?'

'Oh, that's not his real name. His real name is Archduke
Johnnybegood Zig-Zag.'

I should probably point out here that I hadn't driven 150
miles to the NEC *just* to look at cats. I'd never been to a cat
show before, and the idea of pedigree cats was a bit alien to
me. Like my own cats, these animals each had four legs
and a tail and whiskers, as well as a strong sense of self-
importance, but that, from what I could work out, was
where the similarities ended. They lived different lives:
simultaneously more demanding yet moulded by humans
to an extent that seemed slightly unnatural. It wasn't
that I didn't like what I'd seen of exotic cats; I just felt a
bit nervous and unsure as to what they might want from
me. That said, since I'd been signing my latest book just
down the hall at the NEC Golf Show, it would have been
silly not to at least poke my head around the door.

I ended up poking my head around the door for several
hours.

Upon being set loose in a giant auditorium containing
1,455 cats, a cat lover cannot help experiencing an initial
rush of excitement. If I had looked down at the six furry

reprobates in my kitchen at feeding time and imagined they were representative of the diversity of the cat universe, I now realised I had been severely mistaken. Here were cats that looked like miniature lions, furless cats, cats whose insides seemed to be on their outside, cats that looked like Benicio Del Toro ... cats that seemed to have been squeezed out of a tube, fully formed. They all had one thing in common: somehow, none of them looked like they were as happy as they could be. It took me a while to notice this unhappiness. It crept up on me, manifesting itself in a gentle but pervasive feeling of nausea.

'That'll just be all those horrible cat germs,' said Colin, one of the men who'd invited me to the Golf Show, when I took a brief breather to return to the other hall at the NEC.

Colin, it would be an understatement to say, was not a cat lover. I didn't want to fuel his prejudice, so decided to stay quiet about the woman I'd earlier seen slobbering wet kisses on the lips of her favourite Siamese, or the man I'd seen underwrite the tastiness of the cat food he was promoting by shovelling three or four spoonfuls of it into his own mouth. In view of these incidents, Colin perhaps had a point, but I wasn't sure the unusual sensation in my throat could be put down to something as simple as germs.

In our idle moments, Dee and I had occasionally specu-lated about which one of our cats we'd exhibit at a cat show. Normally, we'd decide on Ralph or Bootsy, before imagining the chaos that would follow, as our naked savages disgraced themselves before their better-heeled contemporaries. These conversations were safe to have, in that they involved a purely imaginary scenario. We could never *actually* take our cats to a cat show, since we were fundamentally disturbed by the idea of a) keeping a cat in a cramped enclosure or dragging it across the country for any reason that wasn't of dire necessity and b) putting a cat on a platform to show it was 'better' than other cats. That said, I wanted to believe that some of my preconceptions about the Supreme Cat Show were not true. And the truth was, I met some nice people there, but when I'd been walking around for an hour and did not feel my usual compulsion to own all the cats, I knew something was wrong.

The fact was, I did not want to take these cats home. I wanted to set them free.

Moreover, when they were free, I wanted them to run out into the streets around the NEC (okay, well maybe not the streets directly around the NEC – that would have been dangerous), mate with other, less cosseted cats and create kittens whose ethnicity would render them outside Supreme Cat Show regulations, before finding homes with little old ladies who would want them purely for companionship.

When a cat breeder is asked if it's okay to keep a cat in a confined environment, they'll often reply that 'pedigrees are different' and 'they actually really like it'. During my time at the Supreme Cat Show I frequently heard the idea put forward that all the hoopla was actually for the benefit of the cat, who knew it was being showed off, and wanted to win its category just as much as its breeder did. But while I understood that cats were a proud miniature people, I could not quite believe that their capacity for hubris would extend to a burning desire to snatch the Best of Variety semi-longhair neuter crown from a neighbouring silver tortie Maine coon.

Similarly, the stares I felt from many of those cages seemed to go beyond the normal levels of eloquent feline disapproval to communicate something more damning. What they seemed to say to me was: 'You as well, hmm? *Pfff.*' Did these cats care when their cages were draped in tinsel, or decorated in a *Breakfast At Tiffany's* theme? Did it make their day to be held up above a crowd with a cup and a framed certificate? Did they rationalise it all and come to the conclusion it made the interminable, claustrophobic journeys from Cardiff and Newquay and Ripon and Edinburgh worthwhile?

Or would they rather have not been here at all, or at least have had the chance to leg it around on their own, sniff each other's bottoms, peruse the fine range of high-grade catnip cigars and wander up the hall to urinate on a few golf bags? We'll probably never know for sure, but the body language of the winners seemed to offer a fairly emphatic answer.

So why did I stay so long? Firstly, the shellshock of being in a cat-dominated place in which I didn't feel entirely comfortable took a while to properly sink in. I think I also wanted to stamp this environment on my brain for ever. It was confirmation that there would always be people whose cat obsession had run away with itself far more extremely than mine. It served both as a reassurance about my current self and a warning about the future.

The Supreme Cat Show seemed to be proof that one can't hold onto cats too hard and one should realise that it's wrong to take them away from the dangers of the outside world completely. Most of the cats in this room would live their whole life indoors, spoiled, coddled, possibly dressed up in preposterous garments. That meant they probably wouldn't be found lying mysteriously lifeless on a cold wet lawn by their owners, or get run over by a heartless four-by-four driver, or wander off into the depths of south London and come back looking emaciated and smelling of cabbage, but it also meant they would miss out on a lot. Maybe it was self-righteous to believe that they were all living less happy lives than The Bear, Janet, Shipley, Bootsy, Pablo and Ralph were, than Monty had, than ever Brewer had, but I could not help believing it. And, as I began to believe it, a little bit of ancient cat guilt subsided.

Finally, I think there was one more reason that I stayed at the Supreme Cat Show longer than might have been rational: stubbornness.

When I'd announced to Colin and the other organisers of the Golf Show I'd be spending my time in between signing sessions with what Colin called 'all those folks around the corner who smell of wee', they'd initially thought I was joking. 'Yes,' I'd told Colin. 'I admit it. I like cats.' He rolled this information around his mouth for a moment like a suspiciously tangy crisp, not seeming to like the taste of it.

I'd seen this reaction before – it was only a more horrified, uncomprehending variation of the one I'd witnessed so often all that time ago when I would abandon my nightclubbing allies to befriend random cats on the streets of north London – but now, faced with such a full-on, unlikely intersection of two of my life's main interests, I felt I needed to take a stand. Colin had only met me four times, but he knew I loved golf. Now he knew I loved cats, too. Did he know, though, that, given the choice of whether to abandon one or the other, I would ditch my putter in a heartbeat? Why should I stick up for a sport full of sexist jokes, sports casual pimp trousers and silly headwear? Exactly what was wrong with cats, and the people who liked them?

A grand gesture needed to be made. I had spent four hours of my day at the Golf Show. If I did not spend more than four hours in the adjacent hall, I would be doing cats a disservice. If I could just come back at the end of the day with a nugget of evidence to show Colin that, no, it wasn't that weird for a heterosexual bloke who liked sport to like cats, I would have done my minuscule bit to help the Cat Man's historical plight.

Of course, in many ways, the Supreme Cat Show had turned out to be exactly the kind of scenario that reinforced the stereotypes cheery golf-loving, dog-playing blokes like Colin associated with cats. It was ever so slightly pungent, it was strange, and it was just a little bit macabre. Initially, I'd envisaged returning with a group of broad-shouldered men, all with birdies on their mind and happy tabbies poking out of their rucksacks. This vision had been modified when I'd had chance to take in the overriding female demographic of the crowd. It was then scotched completely when I met Leona from Oxford who, while I'd been admiring her Bengal, had told me that 'you don't get many men here, and most of them who do come here are gay'. By this point, I'd just overheard a lady stroking a Norwegian forest cat and telling her friend, 'No, he's not a substitute; he *is* my child' and I was about ready to go home.

And then I saw him.

I'd been speaking to Trish, a Burmese owner from Carlisle, at the time. She'd been telling me about how it was her first time at the show and she was enjoying it but finding it a bit cliquey, not least the fellow exhibitor who'd peered in her cage and turned her nose up and said, 'Is that a *tabby* cat?' She continued but, as I saw his Pringle T-shirt, I began to zone out from her slightly piqued monologue. He looked to be about my age – maybe a year or two older. Short hair. Sporty demeanour. Cat basket in hand. Bingo! And he was heading straight for me . . .

'Oh, this is Mark, my husband,' said Trish.

So, I marvelled, this was him: the one other Cat Man at the Supreme Show who didn't appear to be bored or gay or at work. Did he, just like me, watch the new Iams commercial and, despite getting annoyed by the woman who says 'I can't get up without my furry alarm clock!' and knowing it wasn't intended to appeal to his demographic of hairy thirty-something, sport-loving men, find himself repeatedly rewinding it and watching it again, just to see the bit where the tortoiseshell kitten does the waggly thing with its paws? Maybe, in fact, he was the real exhibitor of this couple, and Trish was just his accomplice?

'So, you're mad about cats, too?' I asked him, possibly a bit too fervently.

He opened his mouth and just about managed a syllable, but Trish got in there first: 'Oooh no. Mark doesn't really care about cats either way. He's mainly just here as my driver and carrier. What he really wants to do is go to the Golf Show—'

'Ye— Ju—,' said Mark.

'But he can bugger off he thinks I'm going with him. And besides, it's too expensive. He's better off staying here, aren't you?'

'Wuhhe—' said Mark.

And then I took a proper look at him. What had I been thinking? It would be apparent to any vaguely observant moron that this man didn't love cats. I had been so desperate for him to be what I wanted him to be that I hadn't let myself notice the obvious signs: the droopy posture, the scratches on the forearms, the way he held the basket as if it, in itself, might be capable of puking on his Reebok trainers. This man was a picture of unhappiness. He would have rather been almost anywhere than here.

It was time to admit defeat. I slunk off back down the hall towards the Golf Show to collect my books and coat and say goodbye to Colin and the other organisers. I could have stuck around there for a little while longer, but it wasn't really my scene either: my interest in golf was more about hitting balls than buying overpriced Day-Glo polo shirts and ogling blonde corporate promo girls. Why couldn't there be a show that was just one big putting green, full of golf balls and free-roaming felines? The cats could even join in with the putting. It would add an interesting extra dimension.

I'd just started walking to the car and had drifted off into a reverie about this, and about how much of The Bear's rigidly guarded dignity I could strip by giving him the catnip cigar in my bag, when I caught sight of the NEC Golf Show free-entry guest pass dangling against my chest and had a brainwave. I wondered why it hadn't occurred to me before. And then, before I knew it, I was running; hurtling down the hall, dodging in between burger-fed men clutching pitching wedges and women clutching cat igloos.

I found him just in time. Ten seconds more, and he would have slipped into the confines of the Purina One enclosure and possibly been lost to me for ever. It was Trish who noticed me first, and she seemed to know exactly what was coming. She smile-winced in my direction, but, sensing there was nothing she could to do hold on to him now, tapped him on the shoulder. As he turned around and saw me, the sag left his face. Hitherto hidden smile muscles went to work. He was a big man, probably not given to wanton public displays of emotion – the kind of bloke who probably took up golf because the other men in his five-a-side team said he should give it a go – but for that instant he was a rom-com heroine caught at the departure gate in the final reel.

'If you hurry, you've still got about an hour before the Pringle stall closes,' I told him, as I pressed the pass into his hands. I had felt his pain and, for a brief, unlikely moment, we were united. Then, handing an impractically large man-made mouse to Trish and softly mouthing 'thank you' in my direction, he began, very decisively, to walk towards freedom.

HOW TO FEED SIX SODDING CATS:
INSTRUCTIONS FOR HOUSESITTERS

1. Take five porcelain bowls and Free Sideless Entirely Pointless Curvy Purina One Plastic Dish and arrange them on plastic trays on kitchen worktop.
2. Bat Overexcitable Retarded Ginger Cat off worktop with elbow, whilst using phrase involving the word 'cretin'.
3. Whistle loudly, using special Tomwhistle.
4. Open kitchen drawer and reach for two sachets of Felix Meat Selection in Jelly. *Do not* use Felix 'As Good As It Looks' sachets mouldering in rear of drawer.
5. Bat Overexcitable Retarded Ginger Cat out of drawer with forearm. Show Overexcitable Retarded Ginger Cat tiny space between thumb and forefinger, explaining to him that he has 'that much talent'.
6. Simultaneously remove Obnoxious Noisy Black Cat from Overexcitable Retarded Ginger Cat's face and Grey Dwarf Cat from Overexcitable Retarded Ginger Cat's bottom.
7. Gently greet Prettyboy Tabby Cat in unthreatening girly voice, in an attempt not to hurt Prettyboy Tabby Cat's increasingly delicate self-esteem.
8. Open sachets of Felix Meat Selection in Jelly and distribute evenly between five porcelain bowls and Free Sideless Entirely Pointless Curvy Purina One Plastic Dish.

9. Bat Overexcitable Retarded Ginger Cat off worktop with elbow, whilst mocking Overexcitable Retarded Ginger Cat's habit of leaving his tongue out and needling him about childhood traumas.

10. Empty and refill Strangely Named Plastic Water Dispenser, removing soggy biscuits from plughole.

11. Forcefully remove Obnoxious Yappy Black Cat from kitchen worktop.

12. Whistle loudly, using special Tomwhistle.

13. Remove Fluffy Dumb Black Cat's claw from leg.

14. Call name of Troubled Sensitive Artistic Black Cat out of window, being careful to direct voice in way that will not irritate neighbours, or make passers-by think that the phrase 'The Bear!' could mean that there is actually a bear roaming south Norfolk streets.

15. Begin to place five porcelain bowls and Free Sideless Entirely Pointless Curvy Purina One Plastic Dish at evenly spaced intervals across kitchen floor, being careful not to squish too close to kickboards for fear of 'fast-dried gribbly bits syndrome'.

16. Chase down stairs after Prettyboy Tabby Cat, attempting to convince Prettyboy Tabby Cat that just because Grey Dwarf Cat has hissed at Prettyboy Tabby Cat, it is no reason not to eat.

17. Return Overexcitable Retarded Ginger Cat to original dish, clearing space for Prettyboy Tabby Cat.

18. Return Grey Dwarf Cat to original dish, clearing space for Fluffy Dumb Black Cat.

19. Form human shield between Obnoxious Yappy Black Cat, Overexcitable Retarded Ginger Cat and Grey Dwarf Cat and Free Sideless Entirely Pointless Curvy Purina One Plastic Dish.

20. Place Troubled Sensitive Artistic Black Cat in front

of Free Sideless Entirely Pointless Curvy Purina One Plastic Dish.

21. Watch as Troubled Sensitive Black Cat looks up, deep into eyes, with a 'What? You want me to eat this crud?' face.

22. Place Free Sideless Entirely Pointless Curvy Purina One Plastic Dish and Troubled Sensitive Artistic Black Cat on kitchen worktop together, gently ushering Troubled Sensitive Artistic Black Cat towards meaty jellied chunks until Troubled Sensitive Artistic Black Cat begins to take tentative licks at meaty jellied chunks.

23. Refill Strangely Named Plastic Water Dispenser, after removing Fluffy Dumb Black Cat puke from Strangely Named Plastic Water Dispenser's central reservoir.

24. Return meaty jellied chunks from kitchen work surface to Free Sideless Entirely Pointless Curvy Purina One Plastic Dish, whilst making gentle encouraging noises at Troubled Sensitive Artistic Black Cat.

25. Bat Overexcitable Retarded Ginger Cat off worktop with elbow, vocally noting Overexcitable Retarded Ginger Cat's resemblance to a recently lobotomised feline Hugh Fearnley-Whittingstall.

26. Chase down stairs after Prettyboy Tabby Cat, attempting to convince Prettyboy Tabby Cat that just because Grey Dwarf Cat has hissed at Prettyboy Tabby Cat, it is no reason not to eat.

27. Quickly place kitchen roll under Fluffy Dumb Black Cat's mouth, as Fluffy Dumb Black Cat begins to re-enact the video to 'Street Dance'. Use other hand to move retreating Troubled Sensitive Artistic Black Cat out of line of fire.

28. Use Overexcitable Retarded Ginger Cat's inbuilt waste-disposal mechanism on Free Sideless Entirely Pointless

Curvy Purina One Plastic Dish and surrounding environs, whilst retracting all previous references involving the phrases 'cretin' and 'Benny from *Crossroads*'.

29. Use Overexcitable Retarded Ginger Cat's inbuilt waste-disposal mechanism on other bowls to prevent 'fast-dried gribbly bits syndrome'.

30. Open drawer for tea bag and mug.

31. Gently remove Overexcitable Retarded Ginger Cat from drawer.

32. Wipe stray jellified chunk from tea mug.

33. Wipe stray jellified chunk from underarm, but not before using to gain spurious cupboard love from Grey Dwarf Cat.

34. Hold tea bag in front of Overexcitable Retarded Ginger Cat's face, asking, in increasingly frantic tones, 'You want this? You want this? Huh?'

35. Repeat every ten to twelve hours, until insanity commences.

The Simple Life

In his poem 'The Naming of Cats', T. S. Eliot famously
wrote that a cat must have three names. He defined these as
'an everyday name', a name that was more 'particular . . .
peculiar . . . dignified' and the name the cat thinks up for
himself, his 'deep and inscrutable singular name'. I can see
what he was getting at, and it's hard to doubt the nomen-
clature expertise of someone who came up with cat
monikers as timelessly brilliant as Skimbleshanks and
Macavity, but I think many cat owners would agree with me
when I say that he underestimated somewhat severely in his
calculations.

What, for example, about the special name that you
only call your cat when it has knocked a framed photo of
your wedding off a shelf with its tail? Or the abbreviated
version of your cat's name that you call out the window
when you realise that the moniker you have given it in
your flight of early twentieth-century poetic whimsy
('Shimpletybumwhisker!') will make you look a bit of a

twit in front of your neighbours?[7] Or the numerous other
names that spring from some unspoken, instinctive place
on a seemingly weekly basis?

Maybe I'm speaking as an extreme case here: as someone
who works from home, and spends a potentially unhealthy
amount of time communicating with his pets. But I don't
think I'm alone in having always given my cats five or more
names each. By the time The Bear, for example, had entered
his twelfth year on the planet, he could, for reasons not
always entirely clear to even Dee and me, be referred to frequently as Pob, Boobear, The Snufflepig or Doink. And
here we were talking about a rare cat who'd always seemed
appropriately named from the start, completely innate in his
Bearness. At the other end of the spectrum was Ralph,
whose mood swings seemed to demand an ever-shifting
identity and who, besides his 'everyday name' and his 'deep
and inscrutable singular name' – Lord Gargon the Mighty,
presumably – had, by the same point midway through 2006,
been variously known as Prudence, Delawney, Dab Dab,
Scruffles, Tabs, Tabber, Ralla, Ral Ral, Raffles, Tabitha,
Scragpuss, Shagglepuss, Pu Pu, The Colonel and The Squiz.

You'd expect anyone who'd gone through a sex change to
gain at least one new name, and some of Ralph's extra
names were simple abbreviations, but others seemed to
come from somewhere more abstract; a not entirely dissim-
ilar place, I suppose, to the one from which all language
originally emerges. Asking us to pinpoint the exact date
when we first used them would be as impossible a challenge
as asking a person to pinpoint the hour when they got their

[7] Something tells me that when Eliot gathered Munkustrap, Bom-
balurina and Jellylorum together for their nightly kibble, he did not do
so in a terraced house, with a Great Dane next door.

first grey hair or eye wrinkle. Why and when had we started calling Shipley 'Black Mouse'? We couldn't tell you. We just knew it had felt right.

You can evaluate this behaviour one of two ways. Either it says a lot about the personality that a cat owner projects onto their pet, or it says a lot about the way a cat will throw off the shackles and forge its own inexorable identity, whether its owners like it or not. A child will often grow into its name (and I speak as a case in point here), but a cat will invariably transcend it. Much of this transcending will be done in the first two years of its life: the period that, according to popular pusslore, is supposed to count as the equivalent of twenty-four years of human development, before a cat starts maturing at a more sedate four years for every person year.

We felt we'd done a pretty good anticipatory job with Bootsy, whose name emerged as much out of Dee's hopes for the spunky, funky character she would become as from the hints of moxie she'd displayed at the RSPCA. Her intellectual development, however, had been frighteningly, wrongfootingly rapid. Either that, or her initial getting-to-know-you period, when she'd been clingy and meek, had been one great big, carefully planned act of subterfuge.

Back when she'd been Ethel – a name that seemed anathema to everything about her character, even at a point when she barely seemed to have one – we'd been told by Gillian that she needed to be separated from her brother so she could 'find a personality of her own'. And it was true: she'd come across as pretty humble and slight in those early weeks – empty, even. When she sneaked out onto our top floor balcony and mewled to be let back in, pathetically unable to make the three-foot jump needed for safe passage back to ground level, or when Dee found her hanging knotted up in the string to a window blind, only one struggling paw saving her from certain doom, her puniness of mind and body seemed pitiable.

'When I look at her, it's sometimes as if there's nobody really in there,' said Dee.

'Perhaps it's because when you're that small, your brain isn't actually big enough to contain a personality,' I speculated.

What amazes me about the change in Bootsy's character is that all the facts show that when it came, it came quickly, but my memory is of it being a very gradual thing. This in itself is further testament to the degree of skill with which she manipulated all seven of us. Lulled into complacent sympathy by her diminutive stature, we gave her special dispensation to stroll over the kitchen worktops, switched taps to a perfectly balanced trickle in order to give her delicate little insides a less stagnant class of irrigation, moved aside and let her at our food. When she continued not to grow, we chose to focus our attention on that, rather than her steadily improving right hook, her first-to-the-food-dish despotism or that new noise she had started to make when I stopped her climbing inside the dishwasher or Ralph got his sideburns in her personal force field – a noise that could make someone think about the roots of the word 'sourpuss' in a whole new way.

Dee and Pablo had been well and truly under her command from the start, but the other five of us soon fell like a line of dominoes. Certainly, it was annoying that she timed her babbling endorphin rushes precisely to coincide with the most difficult, brain-straining parts of my working day, and it was frustrating when – having excitedly chased the mouse cursor on my computer screen – she trod on my keyboard, deleting 300 words of text, but the sheer ludicrousness of getting mad with a creature this tiny and twisty-limbed made it impossible to see it through with a straight face.

As she jumped out on them like a tiny karate seal pup and saw off Janet, Ralph and Shipley, they must have known exactly how I felt. 'I realise that by rights I should kick the crud out of you,' their crinkled, bemused noses said, 'but what exactly would I gain from it?' When The Bear made the mistake of getting in her eyeline and she savaged him with a playgroup punch, he stood uncharacteristically still, slowly blinking, apparently impressed to have come across a feline manipulator who came up to his standards, if not quite up to his chin.

The observation that 'people don't own cats, cats own people' is a moggy-watcher's cliché, but Bootsy provided a new twist on the theme: she was a cat who owned people *and* other cats. A name like 'Bootsy' seemed to cover her behaviour to an extent, but there were times when nothing less than 'The Pewter Generalissimo' would suffice.

I'm sure that somewhere in her walnut-sized brain she had convinced herself that without her, all seven of us would have all been out on the street, begging for our supper. Yes, I might have been able to go about my day-to-day business under the illusion that the seventies armchair that I'd rescued from the local tip and had reupholstered was my property, but we both knew that ultimately it was hers. Sure, Dee and I could try to stop her from going to sleep in the cleft on the top of it by covering it with an issue of *Grazia* or the *New Yorker*, and, when Bootsy pointedly nudged the magazines onto the floor with her bottom, we could try again, but we all knew who would triumph in the end. Equally, The Bear could convince himself that his favourite computer box – that same one that we'd caught the chicken in, with 'Certified Reconditioned' written on the side – was his very own 'special place', but he and Bootsy both knew that all she had to do was give the nod, and it would be hers indefinitely, to use for whatever purpose she pleased.

I'd seen a version of this before from The Bear himself, of course: the exaggerated fondness for cardboard and poly-styrene, those big hurting pupils, that special way of sitting on your lap that slightly resembled the staking of a territo-rial flag, those kitchen worktop glances that were so powerfully suggestive of conspiracy involving you, him and some dubious canned tuna. Perhaps, in fact, in her first few 'subdued' weeks, Bootsy had been watching him and learn-ing ('Note to self: cat from original batch with biggest eyes and most weedy physique seems to be reprimanded more lightly than peers when digging his claws into sofa. *Interesting*'). In many ways, he was still the master, but, by having the cutesy appearance one might find on a cheap Christmas card or poking out of the pocket of an overindulged heiress's mink coat, she had a physical advan-tage that he did not. It gave her a certain air of unpredictability. You could look at her hiding in a container filled with polystyrene beads and think, 'Ah, isn't that lovely?' whilst simultaneously thinking, 'I wonder if she has a miniature machine gun secreted in there with her.'

So who was the most intelligent out of the two? In terms of questions I spent too much time thinking about, this was right up there alongside 'Who would win in an Ultimate Fighting Champion contest featuring my cats, Bagpuss and the cast of *Top Cat*?' and 'If my cats were the Rolling Stones, who would be whom?' Most likely, they were very evenly matched, and the difference was not so much in the intel-lect itself, as in what it was striving for.

Clearly, they both Wanted It All but, if you overlooked

their general fondness for liking things just so, they defined 'All' in sharply contrasting ways. For The Bear, it meant moments of undisturbed, frighteningly intense one-on-one affection, private sleeping quarters, space to cogitate and countless other, more enigmatic things. For Bootsy, it meant being a priority in every possible way. Going against all feline tradition, she had even trained herself to be non-nocturnal, just so she could spend the maximum amount of time keeping her eye on Dee and me – or, rather, spend the maximum amount of time making sure we were keeping our eyes on her.

I can see how, in the human tabloid world, such an addiction to attention can be destructive, but when you're a pygmyish grey cat with cute boss-eyes and Bambi legs who can't get enough strokes and cuddles, there really is no downside to it. When guests came to our house, the plaudits flooded in, and Bootsy was only too happy to accept them.

'Oooh, I'd like to put her in my handbag and take her shopping!' said our friend Grace.

'She's like a toy cat!' said Phyllis the postwoman.

Even my dad – usually so reluctant to give his time to a creature so obviously domesticated – could not help taking an interest. 'SHE'S SORT OF EXPENSIVE-LOOKING, ISN'T SHE? MAKES YOU WONDER WHY PEOPLE DON'T GET UNUSUAL-LOOKING CATS AND MAKE THEM MATE TO MAKE MORE EVEN MORE UNUSUAL-LOOKING CATS.'

'Good point,' I said. 'You should suggest that to some cat breeders some time. I'm sure they'd be very interested.'

'HEY?' he said, suddenly distracted by a sparrow hawk passing by the window.

For my mum, Bootsy presented no small quandary. On the one hand, she'd fallen in love with her at first sight: she was exactly the kind of physically delicate, sociable cat she'd always wanted, and probably wanted more than ever now, with The Slink's feline dementia becoming more obstinate by the day. On the other hand, when she looked at her, she obviously didn't just see an adorable, boss-eyed companion; she also saw a downy-grey stopwatch displaying the time still left for her to be provided with grandchildren.

She'd always been a calm person, consistent in her opinions, but observing her getting acquainted with my two newest cats was probably the nearest I'd ever get to watching one of my relatives fighting a battle with a split personality. 'Oh, please can I take her home?' she would say, stroking Bootsy, before quickly countering with, 'I don't know how you can keep the house clean with so many of them!' 'Isn't that sweet, the way his tongue keeps sticking out?' she would chuckle, appraising Pablo, before hitting back frowningly with, 'Six really is too many, you know!' I might have put up an argument, had she not been doing such a sterling job herself.

Dee and I had both entered our thirties by now and neither of us had felt the urge to have children – even if we had felt it, our lives had been so chaotic for the last five years there probably wouldn't have been time to properly consider it. However, we had to face up to the fact that, among our friends, we were now in the minority, and that our recent feline expansion had socially distanced us from many of them. I'd always thought of myself as being fairly comfortable around kids, but as we went to visit yet another little bald miracle and the onslaught of nappy talk began, I found that I needed to keep a strict mental checklist, in order to maintain standards of etiquette. This included such key pointers as:

1. When engaging the attention of toddlers, do not tickle them under the chin or wave Ralph's favourite fluffy feather stick toy under their noses, in an attempt to get them to bat it about.

2. When the talk turns to how rambunctious little Edwin/ Dylan/Amelie is, do not attempt to work your theories about 'measuring cat strength being a bit like the football results'[8] into the conversation.

3. Those cat biscuits with the fancy packaging with names like 'Enticements' may work as a special treat for Ralph when he is in one of his despondent moods, but they probably will not have the same effect on a colicky juvenile, and could lead to irrevocable digestion problems.

4. When new-parent friends start to joke about how expensive their offspring's taste is getting ('It's only Waitrose rusks for Minnie!'), try not to see it as an opportunity to talk about Bootsy's preference for memory foam over polyester.

5. Do not spend an overt amount of time cuddling Bootsy, since it may make new-parent friends think you are only slightly less bonkers than Tori Amos was when she posed for one of her album covers suckling a pig.

6. Upon hearing friends discuss the intellectual development of their offspring, do not try to compare it with that of your cats.

This last one I found particularly difficult. I understood that it must have been a remarkable experience to have the

---

[8] Just as it had never made sense to me as a kid that Aston Villa could beat Liverpool 2–1, and Liverpool could beat Wimbledon 5–0 but Wimbledon could beat Aston Villa 3–0, it did not make sense to me now that Ralph could beat up Shipley, and Shipley could beat up Janet, but Janet was still, on balance, slightly harder than Ralph.

minuscule life that you had created begin to make a noise that sounded vaguely like it was addressing you, or palpably tell the difference between an apple and a radiator. But I've talked to lots of parents of 1-year-old children and, in their more honest moments, they'll admit that at that stage they're still pretty boring: quarter-people with nothing really to say for themselves. Bootsy, by contrast, was really coming on, and already had more character than the entire combined shortlist for the 2006 Sports Personality of the Year Award. As for Shipley, his elocution was something special. And what of it if he was approaching his fifth birthday? Jamie, the son of our friends Beth and Frank, was almost eight, and he couldn't even blow his nose properly.

My cats were not children. I knew that. I reminded myself of it constantly, punishingly. They would not grow up to be astrophysicists, or PR consultants, or underappreciated ceramicists; they would grow up to be slightly more corpulent cats who spent even more of the day sleeping than they already did. I did not have any right to bore my more conventional, child-rearing friends with anecdotes about their behaviour, but that did not mean I didn't find endless fascination with the way their brains worked.

It was the sheer range of intellects that one found scattered across the cat firmament that really had me rapt. Take, say, a guinea pig: maybe it has a couple of quirky habits – perhaps it has a particularly frantic squeak and sometimes it gets a bit more of its own excrement stuck in its bum fur than do its more suave contemporaries – but essentially its just the same lovable, snuffly cretin as the rest of its species. Catworld, however, contained multitudes. Even my own small sample of felines ran the gamut from would-be Stephen Hawkings such as The Bear and Bootsy, apparently itching to transcend their physical and communicatory limitations, to out-and-out lunkheads such as Pablo and Janet.

If Pablo and Janet *had* been children, I would have been under an obligation to pretend they were semi-bright or 'just a little different', and that wouldn't have done any of us any good. But a cat – even an exceptionally dumb one – will always look through a dishonest man like he is made of plexiglas. If they had the intelligence of asparagus, it was my duty as a right-thinking owner to tell them so. Being called morons didn't seem to do anything to detract from their self-confidence, and I didn't love them any less for their mental deficiencies, so everyone was happy.

Pablo, in particular, positively radiated stupidity. His development had been an inverted version of Booty's: he'd got gradually fatter and sunnier, without seeming to gain one iota of acumen or cunning. His hopes for an appearance on *Mastermind* were not aided by that tongue of his, which had barely gone back in his mouth since he'd first passed out on our sofa. We'd been a bit concerned about deformation, but these concerns were eased by our new French-Canadian vet, who explained that the reason Pablo's primary taste organ was making its presence so strongly felt was simple: he was missing his main two central front teeth, hence there was nothing to hold the pink stuff in.

When Pablo lay on our bed, there wasn't anything pretty or decorous about it, in the same way that there isn't anything pretty or decorous about a slightly overweight bloke sitting on a sofa in his underpants with the TV remote in his hand. Nonetheless, Dee and I didn't subscribe to favouritism, so we always made sure we took just as many photos of him slobbing out as we took of Ralph beaming and Bootsy doing her picture postcard thing in plant pots. When The Bear dreamed, he always looked like he was in a far-off land, populated by some kind of four-legged master race, but if you'd drawn a thought bubble above Pablo's head in these pictures, it would have contained nothing more than an aromatic dish of cat meat or – during his more pensive moments – a plump gerbil spinning endlessly round on a wheel.

More than a year on, I had expected the thrill of being rescued from feral existence to have worn off, but his sleeping and eating habits remained those of a cat who never seemed sure that he wouldn't be cast back out into the wild at any moment. Where Bootsy and The Bear had long ago learned to discern the difference between the opening of a sachet of beef-flavoured Felix and, say, the unwrapping of a Toffee Crisp bar, the slightest rustle of any plastic or opening of a drawer would send Pablo bounding to the kitchen like Gene Simmons on his way to an encore.

The way he watched every movement of the bowl always reminded me of a centre forward following the flight of a floating midfielder's cross. Would he head it between the goalposts of the kitchen island and the banister? No, he would eat every last scrap of its contents, break wind, then find somewhere to sleep it off. When he passed out on the bed afterwards, one couldn't help but be impressed by the level of relief: that thrill of clean covers and central heating just didn't seem to get old. The only time I could ever remember yawning and stretching with anything even approaching that much satisfaction was once when I was seven and I'd got in a hot bath after my dad had taken the family on an overambitious, snowy walk in Derbyshire and we'd got lost and not got back to the car until it was pitch black.

A couple of summers before we'd adopted Pablo and Bootsy, my aunt and uncle had had terrible trouble with a feral cat. This tyrant had unleashed its outsider's rage on their cats Black-Un, Black and White and Rolly with such gay abandon that all three of them had started emptying their bowels in the bath. Not content with this campaign of fear, the terrorist had brought the battle indoors, prompting my aunt and uncle to install a magnetic cat-flap: a solution of sorts, but not an ideal one for Black-Un, Black and White and Rolly, whose new magnetic collar blocks would often leave them with their heads awkwardly attached to the front of the fridge. No feral had ever given us quite that much trouble, but I'd once woken up in Brunton to find two enormous, presumably feral outlaws fighting in our living room, and just a month or two before first meeting Pablo, an off-white feral tom with a discordant gargle had regularly rained blows on Shipley and Ralph, leading us to a failed experiment in trying to block the cat door during night-time hours.

But maybe we'd got ferals all wrong. Maybe all my aunt and uncle's feral wanted was a fridge door that *he* could get stuck to as well. Perhaps that nasty scratch Shipley had got on his cornea last year was actually the scratch of a paw stretched out in a brave, selfless offer of love. Pablo could get a bit frisky with Bootsy, but I couldn't imagine him raising one of his big soft mitts to anyone. When, possibly perceiving his new, puffy pompom-like appearance as a threat, Shipley pounced on him, he simply took the hedgehog tactic of curling up into a ball – or, rather, even more of a ball than he already was – until the danger had passed.

By now, all of my other cats had intricate histories with one another. When they passed each other on the stairs, they did so carrying the baggage of several hundred stolen warm spots, greedy bottom sniffs, dirty looks, territorial pissings, unjustifiable treats and catnip-based differences of opinion. But as far as I could tell, Pablo bore no grudges. Even he, however, was often on the receiving end of the grudges of others. This is what made his relationship with Janet so odd.

Over the years, Janet had appeared to have little compunction about filling the role of House Simpleton. Perhaps uncoincidentally, he was also the cat whose psychological state had caused us the fewest headaches. Okay, so he puked like an overfed cross-country runner, and this could cause a bit of a problem when he aimed his powerful jets in the direction of the Zenith and the Nadir, the cats' strangely named biscuit and water dispensers,[9] but I knew the early warning signs now, and could usually move quickly enough to avert disaster.[10] And all right, so no other animal in our care smashed more pottery and glassware, and there was that time he'd walked past a candle and set fire to his tail, but there was an equanimity of mood that went hand-in-hand with his clumsiness.

Despite bringing a small forest's worth of timber into the house via his rear end since we'd moved to Norfolk, Janet had, unlike Ralph, never had anything unsightly

---

[9] Zenith and Nadir of what, exactly? Reasonably priced Tupperware pet food receptacles? Do the manufacturers of these products know something we don't? Do dry food and water represent the respective high and low points of feline existence? Or did they just like the sound of the words and not bother finding out what they meant?

[10] If I was in another part of the house and heard a sound like a blocked waste disposal, it was usually too late to save the day, but if I was in the same room and saw him looking like he was getting ready to re-enact the video to Break Machine's 1983 hit 'Street Dance', I could generally manage to slip a nearby bit of cardboard under his chin just in time.

feeding on him, nor had he had one of Ralph's low periods. Unlike Shipley and The Bear, he had never lost a portion of his ear in a fight or reacted negatively to the introduction of a younger housemate. During his leisure time, his tastes remained astoundingly uncomplicated. Where most of his siblings would need catnip bribes and imported battery-powered mice to galvanise them into a brief spasm of kittenish action, he tended to eschew store-bought playthings, preferring to spend many a happy hour slugging a dried bit of noodle or pen top around the living room.

I had no concrete reason to suspect he was brain-damaged. The one incident I was aware of that could have caused such a misfortune was the time when he leaped out of the window in our flat in Blackheath in pursuit of a wood pigeon. He'd seemed a bit woozy afterwards, but our South African vet pronounced him fine, and the lack of inherent common sense highlighted by the leap itself rendered any 'before and after' analysis of his mental faculties somewhat moot.

Still, it would be patronising to conclude that just because an animal is a half-wit, it goes through life without experiencing sadness. As well as being the happy idiot, Janet had something of the dark horse about him, too – and not just in the sense that he was dark, and looked a tiny bit like a horse.

Occasionally, I would catch sight of him sitting on the balcony outside our kitchen, staring off longingly towards the supermarkets on the other side of the lake, and wonder what he was thinking. The answer was probably, 'Me see big water, contain many swimming food, overflown by big flying food, me eat, if could swim and fly and encase in yumjelly, but big bright corporate logos in distance scare I', but it's just possible there was something sadder lurking deeper in that head of his, and that it wasn't just one of his recurring ear mites.

The Bear, Ralph and Shipley had always tolerated Janet – gone so far as to cheerily wrestle with him, even, in Shipley's case – but they'd done so in the way that one might tolerate a village idiot or a former children's TV presenter high on punch at a party. I hoped that, in Pablo, he might find a friend on his level, but mostly they just ignored each other. There was the nervous initial bit where Pablo, now accustomed to Shipley's casual arse-kickings, did the maths in his hyper-aware semi-wild way ('black fur plus cat equals DANGER . . . minus Mohican and yappy, petulant voice equals NO DANGER') then a few cursory sniffs and then . . . nothing.

I couldn't work out if both of them simply didn't interest one another, or if each was simultaneously looking at the other and thinking, 'Check out the *dumbo* – better give *him* a wide berth!' Soon, though, I began to notice a subtle closeness developing between them. Perhaps I took a bit longer to catch on because there were so many noisier, more exhibitionist cat relationships being moulded elsewhere in the house, but it was definitely there. Often I'd find them in one of the house's less frequently used rooms, sleeping a foot apart from one another. An hour later, I'd re-enter the room and notice that Pablo had moved a few inches closer to his fluffy companion, or that they'd begun to sleep in formation, legs splayed in perfect symmetry.

Did either of these cats know what they were getting themselves into? What had broken the ice? Had they bonded when Pablo had mentioned to Janet that he, too, liked chasing bits of dried noodle around the living room floor? Or had Janet simply seen Pablo's ginger fur and started to get fuzzy flashbacks to that decrepit fox he used to pal up with in Blackheath?

Would they grow steadily closer before taking a tenancy agreement on the shed at the bottom of our garden? Doubtful. Would this end with the two of them taking out a mortgage together, or sipping cocktails beneath a palm tree on their honeymoon? Almost certainly not. In the end, they were just two very stupid animals, free of status anxiety or concerns about financial betterment, huddling together out of the cold.

Funnily enough, that didn't make it any less interesting to watch.

What would my life have been like, by now, if I hadn't chosen to own cats? On a surface level, it might not have been all that different. In many ways, cats would not appear to have affected my existence very much at all. I still met people in my working and social life every week without the subjects of cats coming up at all. Within a couple of months of meeting me, most friends would probably know that I liked golf and seventies rock music and *Buffy the Vampire Slayer*, but only the closest of them would know I liked cats. Maybe I had a bit of hair on my clothes from time to time and the odd scratch on my hand, but one didn't wear one's cat love on one's sleeve in the same way that one wore one's other interests. Loving cats wasn't like loving skiing or comic books or arthouse films: when you walked into a pub, you usually didn't feel the need to tell people about it, either stylistically or verbally. I didn't try to hide the fact that I liked cats, it was just that a lot of the time it *was* hidden, by custom and by nature.

At the same time, though, I knew, with the obvious

exception of Dee, my parents and my nan, cats had probably done more to shape who I was than any of my other loves. When times had been difficult over the last few years, it was my cats that had kept me sane. Would Dee have recovered quite as well from her migraines without cats around? It was impossible to tell, but one thing was certain: they hadn't *not* helped. What would Dee and I have done in the darkest hours of our property disaster if we'd not been distracted by Ralph getting stuck up a tree or Janet sitting on The Bear's back? When I'd chased Felix around the house all those years ago as a toddler, I might have been primitive in my methodology, but I'd hit early upon a universal truth: cats *did* function as living stress-relief balls. Certainly, they *made* you stressed sometimes, but when living alongside creatures this fundamentally ridiculous, how could one not keep a sense of humour through life's daily crises?

I felt sorry for people who came home to the deflated atmosphere of mogless homes. I wondered how they survived. Every day, I was lucky enough to witness a miniature soap opera being played out amidst my furniture. Without it, I would have been lost.

When Dee and I had decided to upgrade from four cats to six, we told ourselves that there was no real difference. In truth, there was a very real difference. There had been no hiding the new additions from Dee's parents this time – or at least not without a padlock, a muzzle and a tub of black paint. We also noticed that we spent more time observing our cats than ever before. How could we not, when there was so much going on?

I could assure myself that I didn't go on holiday very often or for very long because I was a homebody or because I was a workaholic, but that wouldn't have been telling myself the whole story. If I was a bit more honest, I could have said it was because I found the idea of putting my cats in a cattery a little horrifying, or that I was worried that, if we left them at home on their own for too long, sooner or later Janet would block up the Zenith or the Nadir with his regurgitated uber-chunks, but even then I would not quite have been getting to the core of the matter. Quite simply, I did not want to spend much time away from my cats.

It may not have always been obvious, but my cats were moulding the way I lived all the time, in all kinds of ways. When, in 2006, I decided to fulfil a lifelong dream by spending a year competing as a pro golfer, one of the most important parts of the planning of my schedule was weighing up how much I'd miss my cats while I was away at tournaments. As well as helping decide where I lived, my cats dictated what time I got up in the morning, how long I stayed at parties, the scheduling of my weekly food shop, the layout of the inside of my house, the layout of the outside of my house.

All this had been happening for a long time now, but since the arrival of Pablo and Bootsy, there was no escaping the fact that I was another half as much under the paw as I'd been before.

My life, much as it sometimes seemed so, was not a game of cat pontoon, and I seemed to have reached a cat limit of sorts. But I knew just how little it would take for me to let my self-discipline slip. This was the eternal temptation of cat ownership: no matter how covered your house was in fur, no matter how much of a twenty-four-hour servant you had become to your cats, it was always possible to convince yourself that there was room for one more, that it wouldn't be too much trouble.

After all, you didn't need a licence to own a cat. You

didn't need to build them a kennel. They looked after themselves, didn't they? That propaganda about cat independence is strong stuff and can work its magic on the wisest of us. The paradox of that independence, however, is that it is also what makes the average, free-roaming cat so much more fragile and harder to own than so-called 'commitment pets'. It's another part of the smallprint many of us don't read when we sign up for the grand Cat Contradiction.

Cageless, leadless and boundary-less, cats are vulnerable to extramural danger in a way that's almost unique among domestic animals. They have autonomous spirit, certainly. Unusually good survival instincts, maybe. But they are, in the end, ten-pound combinations of fur, bones and soft, squishy bits who spend much of their existence subject to the elements, nature, technological progress and the not always entirely praiseworthy whims of mankind. You can look at them chasing a dried noodle around the living room or kicking your magazines off your favourite chair and rubbing their rear end deep into the folds of its fabric, and you can laugh despairingly, but their taste for life on the edge means that you never know when genuine despair will be on the horizon. The more of them you have, the more you heighten your daily joy and entertainment, the more heartache you know you're going to get sooner or later, the more important it seems to make every second count.

So, yes, in summary: six of the little pillocks, for the time being, would suit me fine.

A NOD AND A WINK TO A SLINK:
AN UNCHARACTERISTIC EXCURSION
INTO VERSE TO COMMEMORATE THE
PASSING OF DAISY COX (1991–2007)

Goodbye The Slink
My friend
I never felt I really got to know you
But I've been places you've been
A couple of Nottinghamshires more picturesque villages,
   for example
One of which where car burning
Seemed to be a local sport
And that coal shed at my mum and dad's house where you
   used to hide from Monty
When he was feeling particularly feisty
You sort of perked up in your later years
Particularly when you went deaf
And could no longer hear my dad's heavy feet
Or his shouts of things like
'JO! WHERE'S THE YOGHURT!'
'THAT CAT'S CRAPPED UNDER THE PRINTER'
And 'I BLOOMIN' HATE ALAN TITCHMARSH!'
That must have been nice for you
And it proves that, like Tom Petty says

Even the losers get lucky sometimes
Not that you knew who Tom Petty was
And even if you had
You probably would have been scared of the beard
That he has sported in more recent years
Almost as scared as you were when I took you and Monty
    for a walk
It was a sunny day
In the time before I'd really noticed that you looked a little
    like Hitler
And before the website catsthatlooklikehitler.com
Which proved that, in the grand scheme of things, you
    didn't look that much like him after all
You'd been carrying that feather duster around in your mouth
The one that you must have thought was the world's most
    docile cockatiel
You seemed in a good mood
And I thought it couldn't hurt
A stroll along the lane
Through D. H. Lawrence country
With two furry pals
All was going well
For about 200 yards
Until you saw that Norfolk terrier
And decided for some Slink-like reason
To run straight at it
The little fella didn't know what had hit it
But then not many of us ever did

Eight and a Half Lives

I thought *Notes on a Scandal* was a brilliant film and I knew my mum would like it as well. Nonetheless, I told her to give it a miss.

'I'd leave it six months or so if I were you,' I said. 'Actually, make it a year. No great rush.'

'But I heard it was brilliant.'

'No, no, it is. I just think there might be things that you might want to make more of a priority. Have you checked out *The 40-Year-Old Virgin*?'

'Er, no. Hasn't it got Judi Dench in it?'

'No, it's got the bloke from the American *The Office* in it.'

'I mean *Notes on a Scandal*. That's got Judi Dench in it, hasn't it? Isn't she supposed to be really good in it?'

She had me in a tight spot now. There was no denying it: I could hem and haw, but the truth was that *Notes on a Scandal* did indeed have Judi Dench in it. What was more, she had been indisputably the best thing about it. Like a lot of young men, I'd spent my teens and twenties ignoring Dench, as one might ignore an ever-present national monument, but watching her performance here as a lonely spinster interfering with a love affair between a fellow teacher at her school and an underage pupil had been an epiphany. She was also at the centre of what, for me, had been the film's two most harrowing scenes. These involved Dench, who looks a little bit like a cat and has over the years played many characters of cat-like imperiousness, taking her sickly tabby to the vets to be put to sleep.

It had made no odds in these scenes that Dench's character was an old crone whose craven need for creamy-skinned companionship manifested itself in spite and prurience: it was impossible not to sympathise as she was led out of the surgery, blubbing, or, later, as she dug a rudimentary hole in the garden to put her only friend to rest. You didn't have to be a cat lover to appreciate how these moments tapped into the universal human fear of dying alone, but if you were, you would have felt the force of the grief all the more.

'What about Molière?' I said to my mum. 'That's very funny. It's not out on DVD yet, but it's well worth a trip to the cinema to see.'

There was a time – about nine and a half days in March 1996, if I remember rightly – when my mum's taste in films and mine briefly and perfectly intersected. In more recent years, our mission to find common cinematic ground has been plagued by a fundamental problem. The problem boils down to this: my mum likes films where French people smoke and stare a lot, whereas I like films starring Steve Carell with jokes about condoms. Nonetheless, with *Notes on a Scandal*, I would, under normal circumstances, have picked her a winner. Here was the kind of serious intellectual entertainment that my mum would appreciate, with the added bonus of Cate Blanchett, easily the most mum-friendly of actresses from the generation that, when speaking to me, my parents referred to as 'about your age – little bit older'. No references to Internet porn. No Will Ferrell getting shot with a donkey tranquilliser and falling in a swimming pool. No Jim Carrey sucking on a lactating mother's breast. If The Slink hadn't been so inconsiderate as to die the day before, I'm sure it would have been my first successful cinematic recommendation since *Spellbound* in 2002.

'What about *Die Hard 4*? You like Bruce Willis, don't you?'

'Er, no, I don't think so.'

'One of the baddies is French, I think! Well, European, anyway.'

It was the arrival of the cat known as Big Black Smoke that finally did for The Slink. Him, and the cancer that, for the last six months, had been gradually rendering her a perma-vomiting, matted, punctured caricature of her former self. I imagine that The Slink's first look at Big Black Smoke, in the summer of 2007, could be equated with the moment the herbivorous dinosaurs of the early Jurassic period clamped eyes on their first T-rex. Nobody in my parents' neighbourhood seemed to know whom the devil beast belonged to, but in the month since sightings of it had initially been reported, it had cut a swathe through the north-east Nottinghamshire village of Kalterton.

Normally, calling a halt to a cat fight involves nothing more than a few 'shoo!' noises or a carefully aimed cup of water, but the way my mum described pulling Big Black Smoke off The Slink's scrawny neck, it sounded more like she'd been breaking up a scrap in one of Nottingham's rougher school playgrounds. She showed me the resulting scar on her wrist, and it appeared redolent of heavy industrial machinery. She'd more or less made her mind up by then that it was Time. The cold-blooded murder that shook the population of Kalterton to its core the following week – the same week that I saw *Notes on a Scandal* – gave her the final push.

'I mean, what kind of cat does that?' she asked me. 'Rips another animal's throat out. Can you imagine? Coming home and finding your pet dead on your doorstep?'

Normally, I enjoyed playing Know-It-All when faced with my mum's feline queries. Angst and urine? 'Have you tried Feliway?' Fleas? 'Check out Frontline.' But hearing about the death of Froggy, her next-door neighbour's cat, I was speechless. This was same-species murder, and, as experienced as I was as a witness to mog warfare, I had never come across that before. True, what with only possessing three legs, Froggy had been easy pickings, but faced with a bloodthirsty larynx-ripper at the brittle end of a nervous life, it is doubtful that an extra, spindly limb to flee on would have provided much solace for The Slink.

Big Black Smoke's final act of terror and the image of poor Froggy on next door's doorstep had confirmed that my mum was merely putting off the inevitable. If The Slink did not die indoors, evacuating her insides under my dad's desk, she would be slaughtered outside. One or the other would happen before long, and there would be precious little happiness to be dredged from life in the interim.

I could have gone into the finer details to my mum about why it would not have been prudent for her to watch *Notes on a Scandal*, but it somehow didn't seem fair, particularly in view of the scene she'd not long before recounted to me about her final moments with The Slink. My mum was, and still is, a happily married woman, several years younger than Dench's character, who packed her social life brimful with book group nights, village dinner parties, antique fairs and car boot sales. Nonetheless, when one of your closest relatives has just told you about being in floods of tears 'like a crazy woman' in a vet's surgery, the last thing that will cheer her up is you telling her about a film in which a crazy woman cries in a vet's surgery.

I hadn't seen the The Slink as much as I'd liked to in the final years of her life and, though we'd had some good times – one particularly pungent bag of dried whitebait I'd purchased from the pet shop in 1992 sprung to mind – ours had never ranked in the list of all-time closest relationships between man and cat. We had enjoyed a rare moment of camaraderie about four weeks before, when I'd been staying at my parents' house and she'd jumped up on the sofa next to me, let me stroke the greasy bit of fur behind her ears and hissed approvingly, but it had been an all-too fleeting moment, and the last time I ever saw her she'd been heading for her cat-flap at a rate of knots, spooked by some mystic and – judging from the volume of her purr, thoroughly terrifying – force.

My mum, I think, was the nearest thing The Slink had to a confidante, and it's a tribute to my gentler parent's good nature that even towards the end, when The Slink's notoriously fussy eating habits came to resemble high society anorexia, she continued to keep the diet of her one remaining pet varied and of an unerringly high quality. It takes a special sort of patience to repeatedly buy Sheba and Waitrose tiger prawns that you know will go largely uneaten, particularly when the animal that is ignoring them is periodically puking under your work desk and ruining your phone conversations.

My mum perhaps didn't find the common ground with The Slink that she'd hoped to, but it was a relationship not without love, from both sides. She'd surprised herself with just how thick and fast the tears flowed in the vet's surgery. My dad was also more cut up about her demise than he'd anticipated. 'I'VE GOT A PAIN IN MY HEART,' he said to my mum when she returned from the vets, though he probably wouldn't thank me for broadcasting that. As for me, I was sad too, but I knew that jumbled up amongst that sadness was the sadness of not being more sad, of knowing that I could not be distraught in the way that I would be if any of my six other cats had died.

A cat lover cannot build a special bond with every cat he gets to know. I was lucky in that I had built six, all of which were running concurrently. Every one of these was different, and each enhanced my life in its own peculiar way, but one in particular had developed a special intensity over time. The Bear and I had come a long way since that first night together, seven years before. On appearance alone, comparing the animal that had stolen my chicken bhuna, and demonstrated his unusual uses for sleepwear, all that time ago was almost like comparing a horror movie extra with a lovable character from a children's storybook.

Round-faced and verdant of fur, he had never looked better than he did now, and there was no denying the suitability of that 'Certified Reconditioned' stamp on his favourite box, but he still had his moments of deceit and torment, and it was perhaps to be expected that I'd start dwelling on his mortality more than usual in the aftermath of

The Slink's death. He was, after all, getting on for thirteen now – somewhere in his mid-sixties, if cat years theorists are to be believed – and no cat in my care was more perilously wilful.

Just a month ago, Dee and I had a bit of a scare when he'd developed an abscess on his left ear and the vet had talked of him losing the ear if he wasn't quickly and properly medicated. I thought I'd done a clever job of secreting the tiny pink pills in his food, but each time he would somehow manage to eat neatly around them. The more candid method of putting the pills straight into his mouth, holding it shut and gently rubbing his throat for twenty seconds worked more successfully, until he realised that all he had to do to avoid swallowing them was foam them up into a kind of space dust, then gradually spit them out in a serious of gestures that would have made most quarantine authorities sit up and take notice. Nonetheless, like always, he'd recovered.

People talk about Liz Taylor being the ultimate survivor, and you've got to give her credit; she's weathered more marriage trouble than virtually any other living celebrity, and, like The Bear, had to deal with the indignity of having all her hair fall out. But has Liz ever been chastised by an irate muscovy duck, or had to be rescued from a small spider-filled hole above her own ceiling, or suffered the humiliation of having a furry impostor half her size paw her into her own French windows so her skull reverberates on the glass? The Bear has taught me something about real survival that goes beyond soppy human endurance, with its grief and property difficulties and divorce and psychological 'hardship'.

Three or four years previously, I had added up just how many of his nine lives he'd used up. It was hard to work out what exactly qualified as a full 'life' – I was pretty sure the time he got carbon monoxide poisoning counted, but what about the time I looked out the window at Trowse and saw him sitting on the other side of the river, cleaning his paws nonchalantly, even though there wasn't a bridge within a mile, had a life somehow been spent in the process of getting there? I came up with a total of eight and a half. He'd surely gone way beyond that now. What made his survival all the more impressive was that it had been achieved out of what was, to all intents and purposes, a pacifist ethos. He wasn't one of those cats who went out looking to kill or rumble. To date, I had never seen him lay a paw on another cat in anything but defence. The state of his body told us he had fights, but these remained the stuff of nocturnal legend: screeches in the night.

The Bear lived by a different moral code to my other cats – to any other cat I'd known. Just because he was deceitful and scheming, it did not mean he did not have principles. Rodents – even the helpless ones that my more bloodthirsty cats left around after they'd become bored – held no apparent interest to him, birds were his fluttering wallpaper, and the nearest he'd ever come to doing harm to anything with fins was when he used to gently lap from the tank of Bev Bevan, Dee's old goldfish. His bodily emissions, though often destructive, were never casual or slapdash. When he was required to control his bowels, and had no grand dissatisfaction to broadcast, he had no trouble doing so, such as the time we returned from a three-day break to find the cat-flap locked and him sitting in the bath meeyooping, clearly in the last stages of holding something monumental inside him, where other, weaker beings had failed to. He never muscled in loutishly at mealtimes and when it came to sleeping locations, he was always the innovator, never the bandwagon jumper or usurper.

It had taken me a while to understand him, and for him to fully trust me. I'm sure that, ultimately, he probably still viewed me as bit frivolous for his exact tastes. But a relationship between a person and a cat is about compromise. I'd also done my bit to come a little closer to his aesthetic needs over the years: some of it intentional, some of it not so intentional.

When I had my own minor health scare towards the end of 2007, it did not come as a major surprise: I'd been working myself like a computer-literate packhorse for several years, ignoring the advice to slow down of nearly everyone close to me, and it was always going to be a matter of time before it took its toll. When it did, I was lucky, in that my affliction was nothing overly serious, but it was serious enough to keep me bed-ridden for just over a month. Not long before I got ill, there'd been a report in several newspapers about Oscar, a usually stand-offish cat who lived at a nursing home in America, whose habit it was to become uncharacteristically friendly with patients in the final hours of their life, curling up on their bed and watching over them as they took their last breaths, and I tried not to think about that as The Bear padded my stomach and stared deep into my eyes.

Perhaps he did get off on strife and distress. On the other hand, he was probably just glad to see me staying still for once, and it was just another lesson that cats give you back what you put in. During this period, it struck me harder than ever just how much you could miss about this cat if you rushed into a relationship with him, just how much was truly unique and refined about him, from his falsetto purr to his uniquely articulate tail. Had I ever met a cat who was so

in tune with the two-legged universe? Had I ever got to
know a pet so well, or been through so much with one? It
was debatable.

Of course, as long and bumpy as my road with The Bear
had been, it was nothing compared to the one he'd travelled
with Dee. He still came to me more frequently, and there
was a sense of achievement in how I'd broken down his
defences, but it did not come close to the satisfaction I felt
when I found my wife and our eldest cat ensconced together
in front of the TV or went into the kitchen to find them
furtively sharing a packet of parma ham.

Seeing him looking so plush and content and at one with
the person who had always gone furthest out of her way to
meet his needs, I had a small idea. I'd read about a couple of
annual awards that were given out to rescue cats, or cats
who'd begun their life in tragic circumstances, neither of
which actually involved the unfairness of transporting a cat
anywhere, and I suggested to Dee that we might enter The
Bear for one of them. Not, of course, to show that he was
better than all the other rescue cats. Or because he'd understand what it meant. Just, you know, as our own little tribute
to him.

'It's a good idea,' she said. 'But it has a major flaw.'

'What's that?' I asked, as The Bear, clearly disgusted with
the notion, jumped down off the sofa and shook off the
invisible filth he'd accrued during his cuddle.

'Well, do you not think it could be construed, in a certain
light, by an outside party, that some of The Bear's hardship
over the years might have been avoided, if he had never
been in our care? I think the whole point of the award is
that after you've rescued the cat, you make its life easier.'

I could see her point. The Bear had started his existence
in unimaginable terror, deserted by the scum of humanity on

the side of a motorway. How could a person explain to a panel of complete strangers that, although since that terrible day he'd been poisoned, bounced between owners, savaged, got lost, got thin, been relocated endlessly, lost countless hair, rarely been without an ailment or injury and been forced to put up with sharing his space with an ever-increasing cast of taunting inferiors, none of that meant he hadn't been loved and prioritised above all others? Well they simply couldn't, could they? Not without writing a book on the subject, anyway.

That said, if the rescue cat judges had spent some time at our house, I'm sure they would have soon seen that, within our domestic hierarchy, his status was somewhere about four rungs above royalty. When we communicated his thoughts for him to one another, we even felt the need to do so in the voice of an ageing, demure duke who'd fallen on hard times ('I'm *very* sorry to trouble you, but could you be *awfully* kind and fetch me another chunk of that tuna'). The judges would have noticed that. They also would have noticed us placing him on the kitchen worktop to eat, so not to be disturbed by his ravenous, uncouth contemporaries. They would have noticed us sweeping a marauding Shipley off his feet in order to keep his Bearsleep uninterrupted and, eight hours later, in order to keep it still interrupted, building a wall of cushions around him in order to protect him from a devious Bootsy.

Most of all, they would have noticed the fence next to the road at the front of our house. I would have made sure of it.

We'd had this fence modified a couple of times since we'd first realised how effortlessly and regularly The Bear was scaling it. Initially, there was the bigger fence we had built to replace it: £500 of carpentry that might as well

have been a herbaceous border for all the obstructive good
it did. I still remember my disbelief when, just a day after
we'd had it installed, I saw The Bear crossing the road with
that 'I am a wiry force of nature and will not be stopped'
look about him. 'Have you thought of trying carpet grip-
per?' asked the burly man whom we'd employed to put it in
place, when he passed the house a couple of weeks later. It
was an interesting suggestion, but I wanted to stop my cats
getting killed or maimed, and reducing them to limping
invalids in the process would somewhat defeat the object.
Nonetheless, out of it was borne the idea for the plastic
spikes.

At a glance, you probably wouldn't have noticed these
spikes stuck to the top of the fence, but I've seen some of
East Mendleham's more observant pedestrians wondering
about their purpose – most of them probably just come to
the conclusion that we own a very big, unruly dog. Roughly
an inch long and made out of hard plastic, they're not
exactly lethal, but, if you put your hand on one and got
your weight on top of it, you would almost certainly draw
blood. For The Bear, we hoped, they would provide a pre-
ventative shock, without the subsequent drawback of
amputation. But we'd made an error in our calculations:
namely, that the pads on The Bear's feet are made out of
reinforced donkey hide.

I had never seen The Bear scale the fence with the spikes
on it, but I knew from the frequent cat-sized landing sounds
on our conservatory roof and his mysterious, sheepish
appearances beside our wheelie bins that he did so. He was
a little arthritic by now, and I failed to see how a cat that
struggled with the leap from the floor to our kitchen island
could claw his way onto a jagged precipice three times its
height. The details of his exact method could probably be

filed alongside such other Bear-related enigmas as The Mystery of the Place that is Very Warm and Comfortable for Long Sleeps and Clearly Somewhere in the Vicinity of the Airing Cupboard but Where Human Eyes Cannot See and The Mystery of the Place that Smells of Cabbage and Death Where You Can Stay for Over a Month While Your Owners Panic Over You and Write You Off As Dead.

'He really is a spirited fellow,' the fictional rescue cat award judges would say, having been told all this. Being fictional, and thus entirely manoeuvrable by me, they would have been staying with us a week by now, just so they could get a comprehensive overview and make sure their judging process was as fair as possible. 'So, Mr Cox, would you say that he's the cat you've been closest to over the years?'

'It's hard to say. I love all my cats equally. But yes, you could say that there is a special connection between us.'

'And tell me, Mr Cox, if you had to choose a song to sum up The Bear, what would it be?'

At this point, I'd pause for a moment to properly contemplate his character. I'd think about all those inexplicable fights and how they clashed with what I knew firsthand about his attitude to combat. I'd wonder if the only reason he'd had them – the only reason he ever scaled that fence, perhaps – was because he was defending his five step-siblings, and that, unlikely as it may seem, he was the sort of cat who would risk his neck for his brother cat. I'd think about how much trouble he had seen in his lifetime, and how he was the cat who wouldn't cop out when there was danger all about. I'd think about what a complicated man he was, and how ultimately, nobody understood him but his woman. What song would suit a cat like this? I mean, The Bear wasn't all that similar to Monty, but . . .

'There is only one,' I would say. 'It's got to be "Theme from Shaft" by Isaac Hayes.'

And then, thanking me for my time and scribbling the phrase 'possibly bonkers' in their notepads, they would leave.

TABS

THE BEAR

Shipley

JANeT

FeLiX